Hugo Bergström was born in London England, 1928. He was the second son of the then much acclaimed opera singers Carl Bertram and Harriett Harcourt (stage names). His mother died of tuberculosis when he was two years of age. His father and grandmother looked after him until his grandmother's death in 1931. Carl, unable to cope with his career and two boys, had Hugo and his brother Carol admitted to the Church Union Hostel in Central London. In 1935 Hugo was admitted to the Actor's Orphanage in Langley, where he lived until they were relocated to a converted manor house in Chertsey two years later. The onset of war resulted in the evacuation of most of the boys to the United States of America, where Hugo continued his childhood. At the age of 16, Hugo decided to return to England. He currently lives in Buckinghamshire, England with his wife Audrey.

HUGO BERGSTRÖM

◆

MEMOIRS OF AN ORPHAN BOY

Complete and Unabridged

ULVERSCROFT
Leicester

First published in Great Britain in 2000

First Large Print Edition
published 2002

British Library CIP Data

Bergström, Hugo
    Memoirs of an orphan boy.—Large print ed.—
Ulverscroft large print series: non-fiction
1. Bergström, Hugo 2. Orphans—Biography
3. Large type books
I. Title
305.9′06945′092

ISBN 0–7089–4619–4

Published by
F. A. Thorpe (Publishing) Ltd.
Anstey, Leicestershire

Set by Words & Graphics Ltd.
Anstey, Leicestershire
Printed and bound in Great Britain by
T. J. International Ltd., Padstow, Cornwall

This book is printed on acid-free paper

Acknowledgements

I would like to thank the following people for their valuable assistance: Paula Adamick, David Adamick, Audrey Bergström, Michael Bergström, Daniela Glöckner and Roy Williams.

Author's Note.

Fortunate are those, who from time to time break the shackles of human influence, and are able to truly taste the richness of mother nature.

PART I – ENGLAND

1

New Boy

It was the Year of our Lord, 1935, that I slowly ascended the large stone stairway, half carrying, half dragging my suitcase. Fortunately, the big oak door was slightly ajar, for I would never have reached the knocker being barely six and a half.

'Welcome to Langley Hall, my lad,' a terse voice sounded from the interior.

I peered into a gloomy entrance and hurriedly focused my eyes on an old lady looking down at me with a matriarchal stare. Her face was hard, tough and lined with life. Instinct told me that Matron would be a little fearsome, but also fair and just.

'So you're the new boy,' she paused for a few seconds, and then continued. 'Put your luggage down and follow me.'

Apparently conversation was at an end. Matron had already disappeared around a corner. Gratefully I dropped my suitcase, waggled my fingers back into the land of the living, and with a sigh of resignation followed her at a discreet distance through various

3

passages, doing my best to keep up without breaking into a gallop. Our destination was the biggest kitchen I had ever seen. All the walls were daubed with fresh thick cream paint, efficiently filling any and every crack in the ancient plaster and producing bumpy contours that much enhanced the character of what was to become my favourite place in the whole orphanage.

Matron then promptly handed me over to a girl prefect, who gave me the first smile of the day, and saw to it that I received my tea. I drank my mug of steaming hot tea standing up because that way a piece of fruit cake that I had espied, more likely destined for grown-ups or other people of importance, was just about within my reach. Given a chance, I'll snaffle that bit of cake, I thought. Perhaps the tall girl read my thoughts, for with another benevolent smile, she handed me the delectable slice.

Cor blimey, I thought to myself, this is a lot different from the hostel. I wonder what happens if you wet the bed? Only the other night Harry had wet his. They dragged him out of bed and placed him in the cupboard under the stairs, then made him stay there until morning. Poor old Harry, I missed him already.

'Excuse me, Miss,' I said to the big girl

dressed in strange clothes. 'Do they put you in cupboards here if you're naughty?'

'Of course not!' she replied. 'Silly boys get caned, and what's more, if you are very bad, you will feel the birch across your bottom.'

'What's the birch, Miss?'

'Don't call me miss, my name is Yetty.'

'Now then, you two, no more idle chatter,' interjected matron. 'Take Hugo to his dormitory, and introduce him to the other boys.'

'What about my suitcase Ma'am?'

A semblance of a smile flittered across matron's face. 'You won't need that luggage any more, Hugo.' The busy Matron then hustled us away.

★ ★ ★

Boom! Boom! Boom! The first sound I heard the following morning. The great orphanage gong awoke me with a start. It was very early in the day to discover the first of many customs, which were to become so much a part of my daily life.

Along with the other boys in the dormitory, I was ushered along the corridor to the bathroom, which was situated at one end. One at a time we had to slide head first into nine inches of freezing cold water, whereupon

5

Matron, with sleeves rolled up above her elbows, set to on our backs with an over-sized scrubbing brush. I was told that these cold plunges prevented all sorts of sickness and other ailments. Whether this was actually true or not, I don't know for sure, but I can honestly say I cannot remember ever being ill in those early years. Still, it didn't take many days to become quite adept at missing the worst of the scrubbing brush. One morning I decided to dodge Matron's offending weapon completely. When my turn came round to take the ritual dive, I pointed above her head and shouted:

'Look Matron, behind you!'.

Quick as a flash, whoosh, I was in and out of that bath, feeling very pleased with myself. My glee, however, was short-lived.

'Not so fast, you little whippersnapper,' she said, 'report to my kitchen after tea. We will have to see if we can't dampen your impertinent enthusiasm with a little washing-up water.'

That evening, I entered the kitchen somewhat sheepishly. Grabbing my ear, Matron piloted me towards the sink, thrust a well-worn tea towel into my hands and pointed to a large enamel jug. Inside this jug, which was full of scalding water, items of cutlery were being unceremoniously dropped in by another naughty boy named Peter.

'Now Hugo,' Matron said with a hint of triumph in her voice, 'I want you to use up some of your excess energy to dry every piece of cutlery that goes into that jug, then place it all in this drawer.'

Although the scrubbed pine drawer was at eye level, I soon mastered the skill of slotting the knives, forks and spoons into their various compartments for the night. At first, it seemed the jug never emptied and the drawer never filled. The faster I took the knives and forks and spoons out of the steaming pitcher, the more the hardened criminal next to me kept the wretched thing filled.

Yet during the next few months I became so skilled at this particular chore, it became mine by divine right, just as the washing up had become the right of Peter, better known as Ped. These birthrights, of course, were well earned due to the copious amount of punishment that had to be dealt out to Ped and I.

Ped was a chunky chap, resolute and steadfast, full of fun and freckles. He was without doubt the toughest six year old in the school. On rare occasions he could be unpredictable, but most of the time he was kind and generous. For many years Ped was my closest companion and friend. His first five years of life remain mainly a mystery. If he had any memories of his parents, he never mentioned it to anybody, his dearest memory being his Gran. Despite her old age and failing health, it was Gran that cared for him.

I will never forget the first day of school in the orphanage. After our cold plunge, we had to put on our school uniform. My clothes, of course, were spanking new. Black shoes, grey socks and shorts, a black and white tie (the school colours) and a very nasty grey flannel shirt. No convict ever wore a more terrible garment. Without doubt, it was the most uncomfortable, abrasive article of clothing it had ever been my misfortune to wear. The newer the shirt, the worse the itch. Yet instead of eliciting sympathy, the older hands in the dorm laughed their heads off at my agony.

'Blimey, it's not funny,' I exclaimed. 'This blinking thing is making me itch something horrid.'

'Here, give it to me,' shouted someone. This was the first time I had noticed Mark, and from what little I remember of him, he was a quiet boy who seemed at home with his own company. He was, however, aware of his relative seniority in the present company. 'We all have to put up with this,' he continued, whereupon he proceeded to kick hell out of the shirt, aided of course by all the other boys in the room.

When I was finally allowed to don my monstrosity, minus a button or two, it was certainly less scratchy. And slowly and surely as the days went by, I learnt a few more tricks, such as rubbing my itchy shirt along the radiator. Gradually, I came to terms with the wretched grey shirt. The more it aged, the better it became.

It wasn't the only offender, however. There was another that we were allowed to wear in Winter. Listed optimistically on the school inventory as a woollen jersey, a porcupine quilt would have been a more accurate description. When I wore both at the same time, my life was purgatory.

There were other agonies to suffer as well which came in the form of official and unofficial initiations.

One of the latter occurred at bed time. It came after lights out and we were all merrily chattering away in loud whispers.

'Hey Bergie, I dare you to go and shout 'Ollie! Ollie! round the corner,' ' said Mark.

'Yeah, go on Bergie,' the rest of the boys chimed in.

I realised that I hadn't been in the orphanage long enough to refuse such a request and get away with it. So with an air of bravado I didn't really feel, I jumped out of bed, ran to the landing, poked my head round the door and spoke the dreaded words: 'Ollie! Ollie! round the corner,' and rushed back to bed.

'No, no,' insisted Mark, the oldest boy in the dormitory. 'You've got to shout it out loud.'

I'll show them, I thought. I then repeated the process, but this time I really hollered 'Ollie! Ollie! round . . . ' But that was as far as I got because Ollie really was round the corner and my face virtually collided with his generous tummy. With agility belying his bulk, this good-natured master gave me a resounding smack on the backside with his slipper. And just as I nose-dived onto my bed, he followed up with a couple more well placed thwacks. They really stung.

'I'll teach you to be cheeky, you sawn-off grasshopper, now go to sleep the lot of you and stop laughing or else.'

'Come on Bergie, it didn't hurt that much,' Mark giggled, sensing my discomfort.

'That's what you think,' I retorted, hopping about clutching my foot. 'It isn't the blasted slipper that hurt. I stubbed my bloody toe on the bedstead.'

The rest of the dorm was in fits of laughter.

My final unofficial initiation was even worse.

It occurred while I was in the locker room with a lot of other boys. Suddenly one of the bigger lads threw a pair of boxing gloves at my feet.

'Here kid, put those on and fight our champ, he's not much taller than you so it should be a fair match,' said Dan, one of the big boys. What he conveniently failed to mention was that although my opponent was not much taller than I, he was twice as wide and a lot heavier than me. Peter de Redder, the so-called champ, was the freckle-faced lad I had encountered in the kitchen on a couple of occasions.

Little did I realise then, that 'Ped' and I were about to become the 'Terrible Twins'. Ped was always Dan's favourite though, and I must admit at times this hurt me a bit. This was one of those times.

No adjective would be sufficient to describe the solid, tough, aggressive durability of Ped, who, even at the age of seven reminded me of a young bull.

I had never worn a pair of boxing gloves in my life, and they felt clumsy on my hands. Still, I'd hardly finished looking at them when thump, I received a punch on the nose.

The fight was on. Instinctively I lashed out

with all the fury my skinny pint-sized body could muster and being fast and agile, was able to hold my own. All too soon, however, I realised I was slowing down which is when Ped began to catch me with telling blows. These blows were landing solidly with his full weight behind them. Later I found out some sod had been coaching him. Gradually I retreated all over the locker room, but managed to stay on my feet and stick to the task. I may have hit him as often as he hit me but I am damned sure he hurt me more than I hurt him.

Just then, however, I was saved by the bell — literally — because as the bell for lessons rang loud and clear, the fight, the first of many, was over. But so was my initiation. My face rearranged, I was no longer a 'new boy'. At last, I had been accepted . . . almost.

There was one final initiation yet to come.

★ ★ ★

'All you have to do is make sure you get caned by the headmaster, and not cry of course,' said the big boy who'd initiated my first scrap with Ped.

'Gosh,' I gulped, trying not to look too surprised. 'Up to now, every time I do summat wrong, they just send me to the

12

blinking kitchen, and half the time I dunno what I done wrong anyway,' I told him. 'Besides, I'm not frightened of the rotten cane.'

'Well Titch, judging by your knowledge of English grammar you will probably be caned quite regularly,' Dan cackled, prompting muffled titters of laughter from every boy within hearing range.

'That's as may be,' he continued, 'but the cane is the rule.'

Big boy Dan then rose majestically from the bench with an air of self-importance and as he departed from the locker room, whispered in my ear for all to hear: 'Ask Ped, he's an expert at being naughty.'

On the way to the classroom, I took Dan's advice: 'Hey Ped, what about an idea on how to get the cane from old Birdnest.' I asked.

Birdnest was the headmaster's nickname (he had others), earned by the astonishing similarity of his hair style to the homes of our feathered friends.

'Don't worry, Bergie, he loves to cane us all the time, especially on the bum. It hurts a bit, almost as much as the birch, only we're not allowed to be birched, on account of us being too young,' Ped advised. 'Swearing's a good idea though, that's what I did, I made sure he heard me swear.'

By now I was almost enjoying my new-found familiarity with conspiracy. Certainly, Ped and I were on the same wave length. After lessons, our conversation continued in the same vein.

'What if I say bloody fool?' I asked.

'No, that might only get you a telling off with bread and water for a day,' said Ped.

'Crumbs, that's a terrible punishment, Ped.'

'Yeah, I know, but don't bother because you'll only have to try and get caned all over again. So you gotta say something worse than bloody. What I did was to fall over and say 'bugger it', that's a horrible word and even then I only managed three strokes across the bum, so I s'pose you could say I was lucky,' said Ped. 'I know what we can do! Let's pretend we're arguing outside his door. He usually leaves it open just so he won't miss a caning chance. Some masters give you a choice of punishment but not him, he enjoys caning us too much. Tell you what, you must say bugger off to me. That'll do it, you are certain to get the cane for that.'

I resigned myself to the inevitable: 'Come on then, lets get it over with, I'm fed up

14

with being a new boy.'

The nearer we approached the headmaster's open door, the quieter we became. Then, almost simultaneously Ped and I commenced shouting at each other, and on hearing movement from inside, I hollered, 'BUGGER OFF!' Really loudly, just as he appeared in the opening, his face darkening. Then, with frightening realisation it dawned on me: Old Birdnest may have thought I was referring to him.

'N ... not you,' was all I managed to stammer.

'How dare you,' he blurted out. 'The pair of you into my office immediately.'

After slamming the door behind him, our headmaster regained his composure. And before I could say Jack Robinson, the old bird's cane disappeared from the top of his desk (where the swishy stick always lay in a prominent position) and reappeared in his right hand where it was equally at home.

Had our unruly intervention, though undoubtedly shattering for him, perhaps added a little spice to what may have been a very boring morning? I wondered. The next few minutes were probably going to be most enjoyable for him, which was more than can be said for poor old Ped. After all, the whole episode had back-fired on him.

Snatching a fleeting glance at Ped's face I knew he realised he was going to have to share the burden with me which turned out to be six of the best for both of us.

2

Not so New

'Go on, I dare you!' Oh, how often I fell into the trap of responding to that dangerous phrase, but not this time I thought.

'No fear, I won't do it,' I argued coolly. 'Look, it is no good me asking Miss Robinson how to spell knickers. She knows I know, and besides I would get into serious trouble with a terrible word like that.'

I paused for breath, rather pleased with myself for being able to talk my way out of another ticklish situation. What I didn't understand though was why all the teachers thought knickers was such a bad word? We would often get away with words like damn, blast, sod and sometimes blimey, but never knickers.

Just then old clever chops had a great idea. At least, judging by the smiles and gleeful anticipation on the faces of the other lads, it seemed his notion was brilliant, an opinion I didn't share when I found out what the scheme was.

'Look Bergie,' Clever Chops continued,

'You're the only one small enough to squeeze into the knee hole of the desk without difficulty, and when Miss Robinson sits down, you can see what colour her knickers are.'

Admittedly, his plan was clever in a diabolical sort of way. But no matter which way I turned, or how I tried to talk my way out of my predicament, I knew it was hopeless. I could have kicked myself for having started the discussion about blinking bloomers in the first place. We all knew that the girls' knickers were black, but big mouth clever chops had to boast and argue that the prefects wore navy blue and the women teachers wore white. Doubtless, his sources were impeccable. I guess his big sister told him. Be that as it may, as the smallest and newest bloke in the class, I was the obvious choice.

You wait, I thought, One of these days I'll get even. So, faking an air of bravado, I jumped out of my seat, slipped into position in the knee hole and hung fire until whenever.

'Good morning boys,' Miss Robinson greeted us as she walked into the classroom.

'Good morning Miss Robinson,' the class chanted back a little too cheerily.

I waited for the teacher's chair to be occupied. An eternity passed before she finally sat down. I inched as far away as possible from her legs and remained silent as a dormouse intent on avoiding detection.

Then there followed an unusual silence. Something wasn't quite right. The boys were too quiet. Was Miss Robinson sensing the unusually tranquil atmosphere as well?

To my utter horror Miss Robinson decided to call the register which was normally called only once a day.

'Peter.'

'Yes, Miss Robinson.'

'Robert.' (I thought old clever chops has got a lot to answer for).

'Yes, Miss Robinson.'

'William.'

'Yes Miss Robinson.'

'Hugo.'

No answer.

'Hugo . . . where is Hugo'? Miss Robinson continued. I could hear titters and laughter, only half smothered in snotty sleeves.

'Don't know, teacher,' half the class murmured.

By this time I was close to panic. The rotten blighters could at least have said that I was with Matron or something. At last, the roster was finished and the book closed. I never realised before how loud the closing of a book could be.

Oh golly, I thought, now I am absent as well. Things were getting serious. The tittering had ceased, and I imagined correctly that Miss Robinson's eyes were glaring all round the classroom. All the little sods in their seats were just looking down at their desktops, averting their eyes from the teacher's deadly gaze.

Once more the book slammed down on the table top. The noise almost deafened me as it echoed round and round my cubby-hole. Then once again, the whole room became ominously quiet. In fact you could have heard a pen nib fall on the headmaster's carpet. Why was it that whenever I was in trouble, the headmaster's carpet flashed through my mind. I could see myself standing there now, ready for another blasted caning. That's it, carpets and canings they sort of went together. Just think, that was the only carpet I had ever seen until now, and all I could expect from it was warm feet and an even warmer bum.

Slowly the teacher's chair scraped backwards and Miss Robinson stood up straight and tall.

'Hugo! Come out from under my desk at once!'

It was her really angry voice that was grating in my ears.

'Why were you under my desk, Hugo?'

Her face was even redder than mine, and for a fleeting moment, I felt a bit sorry for her, even though I was the one in greater need of sympathy, considering my predicament.

Then, I had a flash of pure genius.

'Please Miss Robinson,' I stammered, 'The other boys bet I wasn't small enough to fit in the knee hole of your desk, Ma'am, and I was just showing them how easy it was when you came along and then I didn't dare come out.'

Fortunately, Miss Robinson didn't pursue the matter any further. Who knows, she may even have believed my instant excuse, especially as the poor lady must have been more than a little embarrassed.

Soon, however, her usual steely composure returned. Out of the corner of my eye, I sighted a well-worn twelve inch ruler which was clearly about to be used for a purpose other than its maker had intended.

I held out my hand, palm hopefully upwards, knowing I would have to turn it over. I had learned from experience that Miss Robinson was a knuckle-rapper.

Thwack. It must have been the third blow when the ruler snapped, breaking cleanly into two pieces. No one laughed for half a second.

Then the whole class burst into hopeless laughter, everyone except Miss Robinson and myself, that is.

Miss Robinson's displeasure was there for all to see. Without hesitation, she then walked resolutely over to my desk, confiscated my own ruler and marched purposefully back towards me, skilfully silencing the rabble with a withering glance, whereupon she administered six more strokes.

'Hugo, I am very, very angry with you,' she said, tersely. 'You will receive no more pocket money until your allowance has paid me for a brand new ruler. Now go back to your desk, Master Bergström!'

Boy, is she angry, I thought, what with two 'verys' and the use of my last name. I was lucky not to have been sent to a higher authority for further punishment.

★ ★ ★

The bell rang, signalling the end of the lesson and the end of the school day. Ped and I scampered out of the room as fast and as decently we could.

'You know what Ped?' I said, as we hurried away. 'It weren't half expensive, let alone flamin' painful to find out what colour her flippin' knickers are!'

'Yeah, so what colour are they anyway?' he asked.

'Old clever chops was right wasn't he. They're white. Blimey, Ped, it's going to take me ages to pay for that ruler, I haven't even seen so much as a farthing since I came here.'

'Never mind, Bergie,' Ped replied, 'They soon forget. I owe for two rulers and have never paid yet. It's their fault anyhow, they shouldn't hit us so hard. Mind you, she didn't believe your excuse. I'm sure of that. She was far too angry.'

'You can say that again, my knuckles are still stinging.'

But soon I began to feel better, especially after Ped suggested we go and raid the kitchen gardens which were naturally out of bounds. Otherwise they would not have been worth visiting.

⋆ ⋆ ⋆

There were times when Ped and I were as thick as thieves, and these early years of orphanage life were our most friendly. The teachers often discussed their charges over coffee breaks. Later I found out that one of their favourite topical questions was: 'What have the terrible twins been up to lately?'

Old Pa Austin once said it was a pity we

were both too young to be birched. Many times the staff room echoed with laughter, over our antics and the capers of all the other little so-and-sos as well.

Our route to the kitchen gardens took us to a large black shed. Judging by its appearance, the wooden building was well overdue for demolition. The rickety door was unlatched because to lock it, would have required considerable strength and infinite patience.

'Crumbs, Ped' I shouted, 'Let's see what's inside.'

'Sshh, that's the gardener's shed,' he whispered, as he slowly pushed the decrepit old door open.

'It's empty.' I whispered in a more subdued tone.

The late afternoon sun's rays had long since passed, leaving the barn-like potting shed's interior in semi-gloom.

The inside was nowhere near as empty as Ped suggested. In fact, it was full of things, little of which I recognised. On the way out, we each grabbed a raw potato and furtively made our exit.

'Just a tick, Ped, I'm going to have a piddle.'

'Me too,' he answered.

It was while peeing up against the side of the hut that disaster struck in the shape of

Old Walrus, the head gardener. A great big hand fell heavily on my shoulder. The potato being temporarily held in my mouth due to handling difficulties, split into two halves, one half falling to the ground, the other piece making an admirable effort to choke me. Almost as one, Ped and I squirmed free with eel-like agility and ran for safety, which meant anywhere out of his sight. Old Walrus was very annoyed. Even at the best of times, he was frightening. He had a weathered worn face (on top of which perched an old cloth cap), a flowing moustache, large hands, and arms so long that he could tap his kneecaps with his fingers and he was brown as a walnut which certainly justified his nick-name.

'You dirty little thieving urchins,' he bellowed, waving his fist in the air, 'I'll have you shot if I see you in my garden again, by heaven, I'll shoot you myself.'

Fortunately our legs were carrying us quickly both out of earshot and twelve-bore range.

For ages, I steered clear of Old Walrus and his black shed. But then and there vowed that grown-ups were going to find it very difficult to catch me breaking rules in future.

★   ★   ★

As the weeks passed by I began to feel more at home with Langley Hall. I was now definitely accepted as part of the normal orphanage fraternity. The new boy tag had long since disappeared. So much so, that I began to assert myself in all sorts of ways.

★　★　★

Easter seemed a long time arriving in 1936. Good Friday found Ped and I twiddling our thumbs. Then an idea formed in my head.

'Ped, let's cut across the brick fields to the lane beyond the church. There's a smashing stream running alongside, clear as clear it is. I noticed it last Sunday when we had to wait outside the church for our Palms. I wanted a pee, so I waited my chance when the teachers weren't looking, and ran up the lane as far as out of sight, and I swear I noticed some frog spawn.'

'Frogs? Yeah, let's,' Ped answered. 'We can bring some back for our nature class. We'd better find a jar from somewhere.'

Dodging any possibility of being nabbed for one thing or another, we carefully made our way to the brick fields, and without a care in the world, we strolled slowly on towards the church.

'Say Ped, is it true we get an Easter egg this Sunday?'

'Don't think so, who told you that?'

'I dunno. I just heard, that's all.'

After digesting this disappointing response for a couple of minutes, I broached the subject again.

'We get a coloured egg for breakfast though, don't we?'

'Oh yeah, that's right. I think the girls paint them different colours, but they are only normal chicken eggs. I don't call that a present.'

'I suppose not. Ugh! who wants to eat a painted egg?' I replied.

'It's only the shell that's painted dafty, the egg inside is all right.'

'Hm, I know that . . . perhaps it's only rich kids that get chocolate Easter eggs.'

'I had a chocolate one once. My Gran gave it to me. Terrific it was. Do you have a Gran'? asked Ped.

'Not now, she's dead. My Grandad's dead too. He came from Sweden. Miss King showed me the place on a map. It's ever so near the North Pole.'

We were about halfway to the lane, when Ped asked: 'Didn't you ever get one in your hostel?'

'Get what?'

'A chocolate Easter egg, of course'.

'Oh! I dunno really, can't remember. I was given a bible with a green cover, but that was ages ago when I was five. I had to learn a hymn. 'There is a green hill far far away' and then sing it at Sunday school. Do you know it?'

'Only the first verse'.

'There was such a sad picture in my bible. Jesus was nailed to a wooden cross. The Roman soldiers placed this cross on a hill and he died. There was a big nasty storm afterwards, because God was angry with everybody. It's all in the hymn, I think.'

I paused for breath and then suddenly had a hazy recollection that it was actually today that the soldiers killed Jesus. They should have called it BAD Friday, I thought.

* ★ ★

In those far off days, Langley was just a small village northwest of London. There were no housing estates, interfering with the country-side. The little stream that tinkled merrily alongside the field contained no rubbish or pollution of any kind. Nothing to mar the clarity of the sparkling water that trickled on its way into the canal. To see a motor car was a novelty. So it was no surprise to either of us that on our way to and from the church that we didn't see a living soul.

Eventually, we reached the lane, and were heading to the very spot where I thought I saw the frog spawn when we heard a familiar sound. Clip, clop, clip, clop. On turning round we saw a horse and cart approaching.

As it drew near, Ped exclaimed: 'Blooming heck that's a big old horse . . . what are those black things over his eyes?'

'They're called blinkers, the driver sometimes puts them on so the horse takes no notice of anything else on the road.'

'How do you know that?' Ped queried a trifle belligerently. Sometimes he didn't like it when I knew something he didn't.

'Because when I was living in the hostel, my brother and I went on holiday to a little village in the country called Somersham.'

'Where's that?'

'Cripes, somewhere in the middle of England, I think. I know it's a long, long way from London because we had to go by train. Anyway, my brother and I were picking blackberries. All morning it took because we needed a lot. He told me off once for eating too many. My brother said that the lady in the village shop would give us a penny a pound for them. So when we were walking back along the village street to deliver the blackberries, all of a sudden this great big horse, bigger than the one we just saw, with ever such hairy legs, fell down right in the middle of the road. The driver said he must have had a heart attack, because the horse died right in front of us. Some of the people screamed when the horse toppled over. It was horrible to see that poor old horse lying there. We rushed off to deliver our blackberries. The lady was ever so pleased. We got fourpence each. Anyway, on the way back, guess what?'

'What?' Ped asked in a interested voice.

'There was another horse there!' I exclaimed triumphantly.

'No! Was there? Was that one dead too?'

'No, don't be silly. The dead one was still lying on the ground. A lot of people had gathered up and down the street to watch. The driver then got this other horse, which was at least as big as the dead one, and its legs were just as hairy. He backed him up to the one on the ground and then made the poor old horse drag the dead one away up the street. I was ever so upset. My brother said I cried. He asked one of the men where they were taking it, and the man said: 'To the knackers yard.' Wherever that was. That horse had blinkers on.'

'What, the dead one?'

'No, the live one, I can't remember about

the dead one. I must have been upset though, because the only two things I could think about for the rest of the holiday was the poor old horse and the goat.'

'Look!' Ped cried. 'There's some frog spawn'.

Merrily, we collected some in our jam jar before setting off back to Langley Hall.

'Goat! For crying out loud, what has a goat to do with a dead horse?' Ped suddenly shouted, and loudly enough to nearly make me drop my jam jar.

'Nothing really, the goat didn't die, I wished it had for a while. Every time I went into the same field that the goat was in, he lowered his head and charged straight at me. His blinking big horns only just missed me the first time. I only went into his field three times, because the last time I got too near the rotten old thing and he chased me all the way back to the bungalow. Mr. Barry, that's the man we were staying with, said the goat's name was Billy and I was lucky it didn't jump through my bedroom window and toss me out of bed. After he told me all this I kept the window shut, even though some nights were as hot as blazes.'

I think we were about halfway home when Ped asked me about the hard-earned money. 'What yer do with your fourpence?'

'I bought some cigarette cards off one of the old boys at the day school. We used to play knockums and onums every day in playtime. I had cards for ages and ages, but I don't know where they are now.'

I stopped for a moment to make sure I still had some water in the jam jar, and then said: 'There was one time I didn't play though'

'Play what?' Ped enquired

'Knockums and Onums. The time when my brother had an accident with his foot. He limped a lot then and every playtime I walked with him so no rotter would step on his foot. I wish I could see my brother a bit more. I only see him once a month on visiting Sunday when Dad comes and takes us out. That's because he's older than us and has to live in a separate bit of the school. I s'pose you knew I don't have a mother.'

'Yeah I know you don't, but you're lucky. I don't have a Mum or Dad'

'Yes but you have Gran!'

'Come on,' Ped said, as he continued walking. 'It must be very near tea time.'

3

Last Days at Langley Hall

It was surely warm most of the time, that summer in the Actors' Orphanage. An eventful time, a season when, for me, the world became a bigger place.

This is not surprising because from the age of three and half, I had been cooped up in a small hostel in Sinclair Road, London. After living there for two years, the Actors' Orphanage took me into their care.

King George V was still on the throne in those days. I vaguely remember once, being lifted up, by some kind grown-up in order to see the King pass by in his royal coach and horse. These were the days when horses and trams were far more numerous than motor cars.

Memories of my life in the hostel are few and far between, just fleeting glimpses which is not unusual for one so young.

My first introduction to the sport known as 'Tug o' War', however, is still clearly etched in my mind.

Going upstairs one day, I heard the

anguished sound of screaming and shouting. A blend of fear and curiosity compelled me to investigate. On reaching the landing, I saw poor little Tony, another waif and stray resident in the hostel, suspended in mid air. Matron had hold of his legs, while her assistant, tugging in the opposite direction, was slowly losing the battle to gain possession of the whole boy. God knows what poor little Tony thought. Probably put him off grown-ups for a long time I shouldn't wonder.

On reflection, these early years were reasonably happy for me.

But what of my father? Many years were to pass before I learnt how hard things had been for him. And how for eighteen months he had struggled on his own to look after my brother Carol and I. History tells us all that the early 1930s were years of misery for hundreds of thousands of working men and women. My Dad was a single parent without any income.

In the end, he decided on what he considered was the best possible solution. He went back to opera singing with the Sadler's Wells Company and placed my brother and I in the hands of the Actors' Orphanage. It must have been a heart-wrenching decision and I truly admire him for having the courage to make this choice, for it meant he would not be able to see much of us. These early years in the hostel were mainly happy. Being so young, I was blissfully ignorant of world affairs and all the problems that grown-ups encounter. The hostel was my home and refuge for the early part of my life. I was well cared for, and I consider myself lucky to have been there.

Harry, my only friend in the hostel, and I, would often sneak out on to the streets of London, join up with some fellow urchins, and ferret out the muffin man. We would follow in his footsteps, hoping against hope that one of his muffins would topple out of his tray and on to the ground for us to snaffle up and eat. I can still see him strutting along the pavements with his tray balanced firmly on his head, and hear his penetrating musical cry, 'Muffins for sale, muffins for sale,' he would chant, always in pairs while ringing his bell.

For a change, Harry and I would go and chat with Charlie the Organ Grinder. I can't remember the name of his monkey. To me, the organ was a large magic box on wheels, and when Charlie turned the big handle, music flowed out to delight us all.

One day, Harry asked him how he got his lame leg.

Charlie shot a quizzical look at us and then said: 'Here you two, help me push my organ home and I'll tell you the story.'

As we walked along the street, the monkey on Charlie's shoulder, and Harry doing the majority of the pushing, I listened intently as Charlie talked. While I didn't understand everything Charlie told us, I remember the story well because I made Harry tell it to me over and over again at bedtimes.

This is Charlie's story as repeated to me many times thereafter by my older friend Harry:

'I was a soldier in the Great War. Or to be more accurate, a despatch rider in the British Army. Arriving in France, I was issued with a Douglas motorbike. That's the one with an outside flywheel.

'Anyway, communications were often breaking down at the front. I was ordered to deliver an important message up at headquarters, which was miles away, to the rear of the front line. On my way back, I took a wrong turn. It was raining, not too heavily, but a persistent drizzle that made visibility poor and difficult.

'After about half an hour, I was getting very worried. It was then that I saw a foot patrol on the side of the lane. I slowed down to enquire my whereabouts, and to my horror I recognised they were German soldiers. It was obvious I had strayed onto enemy territory. Perhaps my quick reactions saved me. I turned my bike round and before the Jerries got over the shock of seeing a British soldier, I was driving my bike hell-for-leather towards no-mans Land.

'Halfway between the two front lines, all hell broke loose. Bullets were flying all over the place and not just from the German lines either. I headed straight towards a wooded copse which we had recently captured . . . ummm for the fourth time I think. I must have overdone the avoidance tactics because the next thing I knew was that the bike was on top of me and the flywheel was chewing away at my leg. Fortunately my friends got to me before the enemy did and took me to the hospital.

'That night, some of the lads went back for my bike, but it was gone and as far as I can make out has never been seen since.'

* * *

A slight movement from Ped, brought me back to the present.

'Hey Ped, how far away is London?'

We were sprawled out on a path under a friendly sun watching the ants going about their chores.

'Dunno,' he replied. 'Miles and miles I s'pose.'

37

'Yeah. That's what I thought, it seems ages and ages since I was living in hostels. It isn't half big.'

'What is, the hostel?'

'No, London. I was just thinking about an old man I knew in London. And that's why I asked you how far it is. Does your Gran live there?'

'Yeah, she does. Say, let's go see Mrs. Jones. Maybe we can scrounge summat to eat.'

On our way, we had to pass by the staff gardens. When we had free time, the golden rule was to avoid contact with all teachers and prefects, hence our extra care in their vicinity.

'Who's that, Ped?' I asked in an incredulous voice, for there in front of us was a bent and stooped old man, complete with a cane precariously walking under one of the many rose-strewn arbours that adorned the area.

'Blinking heck, he is old,' I exclaimed, pointing towards the hallowed ground where we mere tykes dare not tread.

'Sh..sh,' Ped whispered. 'That's the bloke I was telling you about. Pa Austin. We hardly ever see him now. He's been here almost forever.'

'Blimey, that's a long time.'

Ped momentarily changed the subject. 'My

38

Gran says I mustn't say 'blimey'. She says it's wicked, much worse than sod or bum. My Gran says translated into proper English, it means 'blind me'.'

Ped was very fond of his Gran. She was the only person he had in the whole world that cared for him.

'Pa Austin loves the cane too,' Ped continued, 'He used to dish it out even more than Old Birdnest does. Roy Williams told me once to keep away from Pa Austin cos sometimes he goes around looking for people to cane. And I also heard some of the big boys say he's too wicked to die and that's why he has been around longer than Methuselah.'

'Strewth, come on then lets scram before he sees us. Hey wait a minute, who is this Methuselah chap?'

'Gosh, didn't you know? He was an old man from the bible, who also lived for ages and ages. But he's dead now though, cos otherwise he wouldn't be mentioned in it.'

'No I s'pose not. Everybody in the bible must be dead, 'cos the book is even older than everything in the whole world,' I replied, trying to equal his profundity and knowledge.

We never got around to seeing Cook that day. Other matters were to divert our attentions.

We both heard the yelling and shouting at

the same time. The noise drifted on the wind from the direction of the orchard.

'Come on, Ped. Let's find out what's happening,' I said.

'Gosh, I thought so,' Ped exclaimed. 'That's mad Gerry up to his old tricks again. He loves to round up the littlest kids and then he tells them they're his slaves. If they don't agree, he threatens them with all sorts of horrible punishments. I heard one of the older boys calling it 'chain-ganging' or something like that. Anyway, it's not allowed, but I'm not surprised he's doing it again, 'cos he's a bit of a nut-case. Everybody says he's mad, but not yet daft enough for the looney bin, at least not yet.'

Ped really was a mine of information.

'He's quite potty, you know. He wants to be a doctor when he grows up. They say he once cut one of the littlun's hand so he could practice bandaging it up. I don't think he meant to hurt the boy, but it was a mighty daft thing to do. Gerry swore black and blue it was an accident, but that excuse didn't help him much 'cos Birdnest gave him a good hiding for having a penknife.'

'Look Ped, here comes Albert Jones.'

Albert was the cook's son, a real good egg. Bullies got short shrift from him.

'I tell you what Ped. All we gotta say to

40

Albert, is that there's a lot of kids in the orchard and then we can scram.'

And that's exactly what we did. I was learning the ropes fast. We had not only instigated the kids' deliverance, but we had also refrained from snitching on Gerry. One snitched at one's peril in the orphanage.

★　★　★

November was bidding farewell for another year, and the weather outside was murky, damp and unpleasant. Inside our classroom, we were having the last lesson of the day. Boring, tedious, and perhaps worst of all, it was presided over by 'Old Dicky'.

The appreciation of English Literature became easier as I grew older, but having Charles Dickens forcefully rammed down my throat twice a week by the likes of Old Dicky was a trifle dreary for one of such tender years.

'Hey, Bergie,' said the boy sitting next to me, barely above a whisper.

The voice belonged to Alec Munroe. Apart from Ped, who was my best friend at the time, I liked Alec probably best of all the kids in the orphanage.

'Mmm?' I mumbled behind a page dealing with a character known as Mr. McCawber.

We had to be very careful old Dicky didn't hear us chatting. Speaking out of turn in his class was a crime of considerable magnitude, and the corresponding proportion of punishment ensued if one was caught.

Old Dicky had sharp ears, keen eyes and a cutting tongue, and if all this armoury wasn't enough, he instilled discipline to a high degree with a merciless weapon dished out with ruthless efficiency. Not the cane, but a verbal lashing, always followed up with a minimum of five hundred lines. At least a caning was over and done with, whereas writing lines was a long drawn out affair which often ate up my precious spare time. Given the amount of lines I wrote, it seems that keeping my mouth shut was, for me, always a difficult task.

'Mark's not coming back,' Alec continued, so quietly that not even Old Dicky suspected any conversation was taking place.

'How d'you know that?' I replied, keeping my left eye slightly above the top of my book in order to keep the teacher in view.

'I overheard the Head talking to Matron. What's more there's a new boy moving into our dorm this evening.'

'Flipping heck. I wonder if it's got anything to do with the other night?'

'That's what I wondered. Strewth, I nearly

jumped out of my skin.'

'Yeah, me too.'

I was sorry that Mark wasn't going to come back. When I was a new boy, I avoided him, but after I had got used to him, I discovered he was actually a really nice lad, and I grew to like him. For a moment I pondered on the happenings of the night in question.

That night, everyone was fast asleep. Then suddenly Mark screamed and screamed, a real ear-splitting horrifying sound, that scared the living daylights out of us all. These blood-curdling cries were then followed by a deathly hush.

I managed to pluck up enough courage to emerge from under the bedclothes and cross the room to his bed. Mark was very still, very pale and although his eyes were wide open, he could neither hear nor see me. I was almost as transfixed as he was, until whoever was on duty said:

'Go back to bed, Bergie, he's OK. Mark's just had another nightmare. It's happened before.'

We didn't realise it at the time, but that was the last time any of us saw Mark.

Tim was the new boy that replaced Mark in our dormitory, and being the most recent addition, he naturally underwent the usual trials and tribulations that custom decreed all newcomers had to face.

I secretly admired Tim. A quiet lad, tall for his age and liked by just about everybody. He hated fighting and had the guts to say so, whereas I, who also hated fighting, fought all the battles God sent, through fear of being called a sissy. Later on I began to appreciate Tim's ability of keeping out of trouble.

One of Tim's ordeals was to stand absolutely still, hard up against the wall by his bed, whereupon the rest of us in the dorm had to throw one dart each, as near as possible to his body without hitting him. My dart got too close and pierced his shoulder. I felt worse than Tim did about this mishap. Then and there I silently vowed that this was to be my first and last time I participated in any ragging or bullying again. Looking back, I am sure this was the moment when my unholy hatred of bullies first started to develop.

That night, I did not like myself one little bit.

★　★　★

It was parents' visiting day, and I was really excited.

My dad was able to have the weekend free, after having toured with the opera company for some months. He was camping at Chertsey Bridge for the weekend, and I had been given permission to spend the Sunday with him. Dad was a keen camper. He even had his honeymoon in a canoe, cruising on the river Dee. Poor old dad, he used to sing duets with mother all over the country in the late twenties. Years later, my brother met an old man who had seen Mum sing many times. He told him that she sang like an angel. How I would love to have heard her. After her death, Dad slipped back into the chorus as a lead tenor. He never remarried and he never sang a duet ever again.

I was lucky, it was a brilliant day. Dad gave me a swimming lesson in the Thames and then cooked a meal of sausages and mash, which at the time seemed like the best meal I had ever tasted. It was while he was cooking, that I occasionally noticed him placing his hands on his lower back and stretching.

'What's the matter Dad' I enquired.

'Oh, its nothing, son, just an old injury from the war.'

'Oh, were you wounded then?'

'Well, yes and no. Would you like me to tell you what happened?'

'Crikey, yes, please.'

My brother had told me once that Dad was a soldier in the war, but that's all I knew.

'Well, Hugo, after training in England, like thousands of others, I was shipped over to France and eventually became a sergeant in the cavalry. Our job was mainly to look after the horses and to keep them fit, in order to drag the big guns wherever they needed to go. Without horses, the task would have been almost impossible.

'One night, a terrifying freak storm broke right over our part of the front. All the thunder and lightning spooked our horses. We rushed over to quieten them down, but in the confusion, I suffered a nasty kick in the back . . . '

'Poor old Dad.'

'Actually Hugo, my mates said I was lucky, because I had to go to hospital behind enemy lines, and as a result I managed to miss the rest of the war. But this all happened many years ago. There is nothing for you to worry about now.'

Little did my father know that his old war injury was to be further aggravated during Britain's next confrontation with Germany.

★ ★ ★

Early January at Langley Hall was a hive of activity, for it was the time of the annual pantomime, which was always rehearsed in our own Bijou Theatre, situated beneath the girls living quarters. Both the girls' and the boys' living quarters were extensions to the main Georgian building.

The event was always very important. This year we were performing Cinderella at the Gaiety Theatre in London's West End. Although my age group were small fry and our parts did not take much learning, we still had to be present at most of the rehearsals. Fate decreed that in my first panto, I was to be one of the green-clad elves manning a two-man saw. Ped, of course, was the other elf.

January 12th, 1937 is a date I remember well, for this was the day of the premier performance.

All of us elves were assembled in our respective places. The curtain was raised for the first scene to the music of Debroy Summers and his band. A hush fell gently over the whole house, then Ped and I commenced proceedings by starting to cut the log.

Then, disaster struck. Despite all the rehearsals we had been through, we both pushed the damn saw at the same time, and, of course, to remedy this catastrophic situation, instinctively we both pulled a fraction of a second later. Needless to say, we finally got our act together and my life's first embarrassing moment became history.

★ ★ ★

The winter finally surrendered to that sweetest of all seasons, Spring. Inevitably the vast expanses of the neighbouring brick fields beckoned us to come and explore. Bread and cheese were plentiful in the hedgerows and emerging gooz-gogs (fresh young dandelion leaves) were beginning to compete for territory with the other wild plant life.

It was on such a day, while out with some of my companions, that our meanderings took us right up to the canal. It was then we saw two of our older boys heading our way, and in hot pursuit were a bunch of villagers obviously hell bent in giving them both a beating.

On seeing us, Bruce shouted: 'Run back to Langley Hall before you get hurt,' and then he and his friend plunged into the canal.

We all fled as fast as we could. Bruce and the other prefect caught us up.

Meanwhile, the village kids halted at the canal and started shooting at us with their air guns and catapults. I was hit up the backside, luckily with a pellet almost spent in flight, but two of our kids who were a trifle slower, picked up several battle wounds in the form of several small red swellings.

Next day, after lessons, a council of war was convened.

Although often out-numbered, we usually outsmarted our opponents, and the coming fracas was one of our most noteworthy battles. The war party was organised into two main bands. All of us tykes were to occupy the roof of the old cricket pavilion, which overlooked the tall brick wall separating the orphanage grounds from the street. We were armed to the teeth with bucketfuls of stones.

The older group went out as decoys, to lure the village kids within our range. The plan worked beautifully. The Pavilion roof gave us a height advantage, while the huge brick wall dividing the school from the road provided us with complete safety. Needless to say, with these two significant strategic advantages, we were able to win the day.

It is true to say that our skirmishes with the villagers were an ongoing and never-ending affair. This one, being of a more serious nature, however, soon became known to the authorities on both sides of the wall. The result was a period of time of confinement to the orphanage grounds and a liberal dose of caning for many of the boys.

One other event comes to mind, one that occurred under the tyrannical rule of our headmaster, Old Birdnest. One evening, prior to bed-time, four restless boys from the same dormitory decided to play a prank. Which one of the four had the whim, I have no idea. Nor does it matter. But he was looking at a red bucket, and from that casual glance developed a full-blown practical joke.

Now, a pre-World War Two empty fire bucket is an object weighing a few pounds. If the same container is filled with, say, half full of water, it becomes considerably heavier. Now if one balances this same fire bucket, half filled with water on the top of a door that is slightly ajar, I think it would be fair to say, the pail would then be a lethal weapon, with potential to cause painful and serious injury, especially if it were to fall onto a boy's head.

I knew all four of these boys, Roy, Arthur, John and Doug, and I can promise you they were jolly good chaps. But at this moment in their upbringing, like all of us from time to time, they didn't stop to think. They were carried away by their own enthusiasm, with what they thought would be a brilliant joke, to try out on the first unfortunate lad who unwittingly entered the dormitory.

The scene was set. The four youngsters dressed in their pyjamas, sitting on the edge of their beds, all waiting with bated breath, to see who would be the unlucky person who would next walk through the door to receive a thorough soaking.

Alas, it was Matron! For what reason she entered the room at this untimely and unexpected moment, I don't know. But fate's choice of a victim was not a happy one for the boys.

By some miracle, only the water cascaded down upon her lean frame. The bucket came crashing down beside her, creating a noisy and frightening din, causing poor old Matron not only to splutter and choke, but also to jump about four feet in the air. The boys, of course, had not only failed to see the dangerous side to this whimsical monkey-trick, but to their eternal credit not one wished or expected that Matron would be the victim of their masterly ploy.

It was a cold shower for Matron but there was hot water in store for four boys.

When Matron finally composed herself, she glared round the room, anger written all over her face, and with a withering tongue lashed out a verbal onslaught which ended only when four boys stood smartly to attention outside the headmaster's study waiting for what they must have known was going to be a rough ordeal.

★ ★ ★

Often, when we assumed a caning was imminent, if we had time to spare, we would slip on an extra pair of underpants, in order to give our bottoms that little extra cushioning, and by so doing hoping to alleviate at least some of the pain of the cane. Sadly, these four boys were in their pyjamas and what with matron in such close attendance had no chance of adding any packaging to the necessary part of their anatomy.

The practical jokers were to enter the study one at a time, for a hiding that may have ranked as one of the orphanage's best or worst, depending on which side of the fence your sympathy lay. While Arthur was in the room, the other three were counting the strokes, a pastime if for no other reason, kept you mentally occupied until your own turn came round.

The canings were severe, and for many days the lads bore black and blue marks. Later on, a rumour started circulating round the dorms and forms that suggested in future the cane should not be raised above the level of the shoulder. A rule which at a later date, Doug was to point out to a teacher, who was encroaching too much height before delivery.

The cane was very widely used and not only by Pa and the headmaster. Other teachers often liked to assert their power as well. Before Bomber Howells, our sports master, became married, Saturday mornings were known as 'The Reign of Terror'.

Fortunately, marriage mellowed the man, and by the time we all moved to Silverlands we classed him as a good teacher, especially when coaching us at cricket. But in his days as a bachelor, 'Wow'.

Saturday mornings was the 'Time of Infliction', and very few boys from the third and fourth forms escaped regular canings. Even one or two of us in form two were unlucky enough to occasionally share their misfortune.

However, the big stick was not just the prerogative of the masters. The bully boy prefects at the top of the school struck fear into us Ticks ('Tick' was a favourite nickname for any boy small enough to be bullied).

One of their favourite pastimes was known as 'The Rising Sun'. This involved grabbing a boy who for want of a better phrase wasn't flavour of the week, de-bagging him and forcing the ill-fated lad to face downwards on a table, and then taking turns in smacking the luckless victim on his bottom until his posterior glowed a scarlet red.

★ ★ ★

The death of the president Sir Gerald du Maurier in the year 1936 marked the end of an era. The engagement of the more liberal Noel Coward, as the new president of the Actors' Orphanage brought about many improvements, and indeed the sun started to set on some of the Dickensian practices. A few teachers of the old brigade including the headmaster himself suddenly vanished from the scene. The segregation of the sexes gradually disintegrated and by the year 1939 co-education was in full swing. The reasons behind all these progressive changes, were of course, unknown to boys not quite ten years old and younger.

Despite this progressive liberalisation, however, as odd as it may seem, I for one was to endure even more canings at Silverlands than I received at Langley Hall. This was probably due to my ever-increasing rebellious attitude towards authority, which later on in life, was to be one of my major problems in His Majesty's employ. I must say though, I had no reasonable cause for complaint regarding my increasing share of punishment, for I surely deserved it. For me, caning was a far less devastating punishment than having my ration of jam for the teatime meal confiscated.

★　★　★

In the late 1930s, it was true to say that certain unsavoury Victorian practices were on the decline, but our new headmaster held them intact for as long as possible. No time at all was lost before Old Ruggles (for that was the name we had given to the new headmaster) began to assert himself in every way possible.

One day Granville had once again upset Old Ruggles. Gran was a relatively senior boy of 12 years old, of medium build, blond hair and blue eyes. A likeable chap, not a bully by any means, but very persuasive, he would like to organize events that he deemed to be under his personal jurisdiction. Poor old Granny was having a rough passage of late, an experience not unknown to many of us from time to time. He was three years older than me, and far more experienced in the orphanage way of life, having already endured the last eight years in Langley Hall. As a veteran of twelve years old, three quarters of his total life span had been spent in the orphanage which meant that his knowledge of this kind of life was considerable.

Granny was rather fond of gob-stoppers, but he knew better than to risk going to the village himself, because Old Ruggles had previously gated him for some minor misdemeanour. Now discovery beyond the borders of the orphanage would have resulted in several strokes of the cane. So he looked round for a younger boy to run an 'Errand of Mercy' which meant bringing him back some gob-stoppers.

Just by chance Granny had espied Tiny Tony, a lad very new to the orphanage. His opportunity had arrived.

'Hello Tony, will you do me a favour, and nip down to the village shop for me, and buy three penneth of gob-stoppers? You can have one for your trouble, provided you're quick.'

It was a mystery to many of us how Granny always seemed to have enough pennies to buy his gob-stoppers.

It is vital for any new boy to show a reasonable willingness towards an older boy of many years standing, if only for reasons of self preservation. So, without further ado, Tony set off to fetch the sweets.

Now, our new headmaster had a talent that once or twice cost me dear. He thoroughly enjoyed looking out from various vantage points with the aid of a very good pair of binoculars, with the sole purpose of discovering if there were any boys or girls being naughty enough to reprimand. His expertise in his devious hobby, enabled him to bag enough victims to satisfy his lustful desires in the caning department.

Inevitably little Tony was seen by Old Ruggles coming through the main gate carrying a white paper bag clutched tightly in his hand. This in itself is not all that incriminating. However, Tony was very young, very new and very small: three excellent reasons why he should not have been alone in the village in the first place.

'Come here boy,' said the headmaster who had quickly intercepted little Tony. 'What is your name?' he continued.

'Tony, sir' came the reply, with more than a hint of alarm showing on his face.

'Well, Tony, what have you in the bag?'

'They're gob-stoppers, Sir.'

'Are they indeed, and where, I might ask, did you find enough money to buy all those gob-stoppers?'

'The money wasn't mine, Sir. Granville asked me to go and buy three penneth for him. Only one of them is for me.'

'Oh, is that so? My, my, that's a pity, for I must not only confiscate all the ghastly sweets, but you will now go and run an errand for me. Tell Master Granville to report to my study at once.'

On Gran's arrival at the headmaster's study the angry Old Ruggles waded straight in.

'Granville, what is the meaning of sending out for sweets when I had previously confined you to the premises?'

'Sir. Tony Perritt had not been gated. Otherwise I would not have asked him.'

'Don't be flippant with me, young man,' Old Ruggles continued. 'The whole purpose of being confined to the Hall is to stop all privileges from outside.'

'But I didn't know this, Sir.' Gran had now crossed the rubicon, a caning was now a certainty.

'Don't argue with me, Granville,' said the now exasperated headmaster, who then proceeded to cane the lad.

Old Ruggles was very proud of his cane. To be accurate it was not really a cane. As far as I remember, the weapon was an army officer's stick. I was told that this stick had a lead insert, and was lined and covered with leather. This may or may not be true, but in any event it hurt.

Now Gran was not only hurt physically. The injustice of the whole unfortunate affair was more than he was willing to accept, and on a sudden impulse he snatched his hand away just in time to elude the third blow and ran quickly out of the study. From what I could gather, no more of this matter was mentioned, and after this incident both Gran and Ruggles were far more amenable to each other. Perhaps Old Ruggles realised he had been too hard on poor Granny.

★ ★ ★

But I must be fair to all the staff and authorities in general. From the time Noel Coward took over the presidency, I am sure that the Actors' Orphanage became as good as, if not better than any other orphanage in the land.

Among the myriad of improvements initiated by the Actors' Orphanage committee, under the direction of Noel Coward, was its relocation to Silverlands in Chertsey. It was decided that Langley Hall was no longer appropriate and that Silverlands would be a far more suitable place for all concerned.

I remember the buzz of excitement in those last few days before being transported to our new home in the Surrey countryside.

4

Silverlands

Silverlands was situated in the heart of the Surrey countryside, a place of beauty with acres of private woodlands and fields. In days long past, the area surrounding Silverlands consisted mainly of forests and pastureland. Early in the fifteenth century, the whole vast territory was recorded as Silverlond. The house itself was a magnificent mansion, built in the first half of the nineteenth century. The cobbled courtyard and stables were rather less grand, and in our time, had been converted into the boys' and girls' locker rooms, plus one or two outhouses.

Many were the reasons for us leaving Langley Hall and moving to Silverlands in 1938. One reason being the need to expand, the other being the impending possibility of war with Germany. Also Noel Coward had knowledge of the spaciousness of Silverlands, and the good sense to realize its potential.

For many a day the thrill of exploration into unknown regions filled me with joy. And when I wanted to free myself from the shackles of authority, these picturesque woodlands became my escape route to peace and solitude.

I used to wonder whether there were any ghosts haunting the place, but then I reasoned that if there were any ghosts, they surely wouldn't hang around, now that seventy odd noisy children of all ages had invaded their domain. Nor did anyone ever report any mysterious or unexplained happenings, so if the place had ever been inhabited by disembodied spirits, they certainly didn't make themselves known above the din.

Despite the splendour of Silverlands, however, and all its promise of a bright shiny future, our time there was nevertheless marred at times with sadness, despair and the occasional disaster.

★ ★ ★

Being a wild bunch of boys and girls — most of us from broken homes or at the very least, semi-orphaned — ambulances were a common sight at our front entrance.

I remember poor old Fitz. His real name was Peter Parker.

One day, he managed to secretly get hold of a chair to make a sleigh. A harmless enough plan, you'd think. Yet, while trying to extricate one of the wooden rods from the chair-back, he jerked it straight up into his eye which fell out of its socket, damaged beyond repair.

My brother Carol was with Fitz when he injured himself. He heard Fitz cry out, and on seeing his pal in such a terrible state, very nearly passed out. He was however able to keep sufficient presence of mind to shout for help.

As for me, I was wandering around outside the front at the time when I saw an ambulance come screaming up the drive and back up to the entrance. Moments later, I saw poor old Fitz being carried out on stretcher. He must have been in a lot of pain because I could hear him moaning.

Another episode I can still recall vividly left me feeling very sad.

A few of us were playing a game of monopoly in the recreation room one day when a little tiff developed between Ped and I. Then, all of a sudden, Ped hurled himself across the table, monopoly money flying all over the place, and started fighting me.

I in turn became angry and disappointed, because I did not expect to have to fight my best friend. All the other boys were enjoying the fight. I for one was glad when the bell rang and our fracas came to an end.

At about this time we had a teacher, Mr. Simpson, who was respected and looked up to by everybody. He had a way of making me feel special.

I remember one day in particular though, when I was sitting under the big horse chestnut and Mr. Simpson was giving us a history lesson. I was enthralled, even more so when he allowed the subject to digress into a nature lesson. His knowledge of the wildlife surrounding Silverlands, impressed me no end. So much so that I was hoping he wouldn't get fed up with me asking him so many questions.

Then, for a brief moment, he turned away. I noticed out of the corner of my eye, his face, normally so handsome, was contorted in pain.

The memory of that moment still haunts me. A cold shiver passed through my body. Somehow I knew then with utter certainty that I was going to lose a good friend.

After the lesson I stayed until the other boys had gone.

'Please, Mr. Simpson, are you all right?' I asked.

'Oh, it's just a tummy ache, Hugo, I'll be fine tomorrow.'

Our eyes met and he patted me on my head. 'I am glad you like nature, Hugo. But always remember, history is also a very important subject.'

That was the last time I ever saw Mr. Simpson.

Within a few days, my favourite teacher died of stomach cancer. He was just twenty-four years old.

★ ★ ★

On another occasion, I entered the common room one morning and saw Ped holding a crumpled letter in his hand. On the large heavy table beside him lay an envelope edged in black.

Ped had tears in his eyes, a sight I'd never seen before and never saw again. He had just received news that his Gran had died. There he was, yet another nine year-old having to stand fast through adversity alone. Gran was his last and only memory of someone who loved him.

★ ★ ★

Autumn was with us and the squirrels in the woods were a flurry of activity gathering nuts before the onrush of winter. Naturally, I was obsessed with conkers which were an essential part of our early winters.

'Look Ped, if we wait till the weekend there won't be any blinking conkers left. I say we get up very early tomorrow morning, long before breakfast, climb out through our dormitory window and sneak off to the paddock. This way we can have first choice and pick out all the best conkers.'

'Good idea,' said Ped, 'but we'd better not get caught 'cos we're not allowed up and out till seven.'

I knew that but decided no further comment was necessary. Besides it would be as easy as peeing up a wide road. No one in their right mind would be looking for a couple of boys slithering down a drainpipe and running across the front lawns that early in the morning. Or so I thought.

That night I went to bed feeling intensely happy, dreaming about all the possible ways I could harden off my conkers. I remember lying in bed and thinking: 'Wonder if I can get round Cook and get her to bake some. No, she would never agree. I know, I'll nip off to dear old Mrs. Hazel at the bungalow, I'll pinch a couple of flowers from the gardens (musn't be seen though or else everyone will call me a sissy) and take them to Mrs. H as a present. Sure as eggs are eggs, she will bake my conkers, and they'll be as hard and tough as any in the school.' I was nothing if not ambitious.

Next thing I remember, Jason was calling us to hurry up. We had to let him in on our secret because he slept by the window.

As it turned out, both Ped and I were surprised how easy it was to get to the ground. The Virginia creeper certainly helped us. We scampered off to the paddock and collected pocketfuls of the most gorgeous creamy brown conkers you ever saw.

★ ★ ★

It was Friday. At quarter to nine, we all trooped into the assembly room for prayers and notices.

Usually I found this a very boring part of my day. For one thing, I had to sit still too long, all of ten minutes. What's more, most of the time I never understood what the masters and mistresses were talking about, mainly because I wasn't listening. But I do remember the ceiling. As some woman teacher droned on saying how naughty we all were, my eyes would wander upwards over the vast ceiling picking out all the different carvings.

But this particular morning I was brought back to earth with a bump.

'Will the two boys who were seen climbing out of their dormitory window before breakfast this morning report to my study immediately after assembly,' the headmaster said.

Cor blimey, I thought. What a change of heart. Barely has he finished saying: 'May Jesus Christ have mercy on us all,' than he's itching to get his hands on his cane and whack our backsides. I sensed Ped tighten up beside me.

'How did old Ruggs find out?' I asked Ped.

'Probably a girl,' said Ped shrugging his shoulders in resignation. Slowly we made our way down the corridor. I looked at Ped and, as usual when in trouble, his face was infuriatingly blank. Leaving the headmaster's study ruefully rubbing our bums, he said: 'Strewth, we didn't half get off lightly. I expected at least six of the best.'

I was still musing over who could have possibly reported us, when he added: 'You know, when we reached the ground this morning, I could have sworn I saw a face at the girl's dormitory window. I wonder if one of the girls snitched on us?'

***

By now all the children had entered their various classrooms scattered higgledy-piggledy all through the buildings and outhouses.

To this day I will never understand how we found ourselves in the girl's locker room.

'Look Ped, this room is so tidy. Just look at all these wellies standing neatly in a row. Just like a lot of soldiers on parade, they are. Same as that picture we saw in the War Illustrated the other day. Hey Ped, what the blazes are you doing?'

Ped turned round with a broad grin splitting his freckled face from ear to ear. In his stubby fingers raised high above his head he was brandishing a gleaming pair of scissors. The glint in his bright blue eyes seized me.

'Crikey, do they cut?' I cried.

Ped tentatively snipped at one of the wellington boots. Snip, snip, snip. What a smashing little game this was. The cuts became longer as we tried to outdo each other. The rubber parted so smoothly and satisfyingly between the scissors' blades. In no time at all, a goodly proportion of girls' wellies lay in shreds and tatters. Bits and pieces were haphazardly strewn all over the locker room.

Suddenly, we heard the sound of footsteps.

'Quick Ped, run for it, someone's coming.'

In a flash, we scurried out into the open, dodged round the corner of the courtyard and hid behind the coal bunker. There we waited not daring to move a muscle, hoping the oncoming footsteps wouldn't stop, but carry on and fade away into the distance which, to our mutual delight and relief, they did.

Now the enormity of our crime was just beginning to seep into my mind. My conscience was starting to tell me we had both been stupid and bad. What on earth possessed us? I thought. After all, it's not even certain that the girls did tell on us. In fact, it was more likely that Ruggles had spotted us through his trusty binoculars.

'Ped, I've just been wondering. Do you think its possible that old Ruggs had his binoculars on us? Perhaps the girls didn't tell on us after all.'

'Come on, Bergie, what's done is done. Let's get back to the classroom and say nothing at least for the time being,' Ped replied.

Yet I could tell he was just as worried as I was.

'OK,' I mumbled, not quite sure what he meant by 'the time being.'

On entering our class, we walked sheepishly to our desks and sat down trying to keep as low a profile as possible.

'Good heavens above! So the early birds have found time to attend our English lesson after all.' The teacher's words were clear and concise as usual. I think he always felt it his duty to instil the brilliance of his wit onto even the youngest of us.

'Are you sure that both of you are quite comfortable sitting down on your posteriors, or would you like to stand?' he continued.

Ha Ha Ha! What a joker, I thought.

Naturally the rest of the boys in the classroom found the teacher's remarks amusing.

But Ped and I were in no mood to share their fun. We were far too worried to appreciate his eloquent sarcasm. So we just slunk deeper into our seats and were perfect pupils for the rest of the period.

★　★　★

It was at break time that the storm broke. Above the usual school din, we could hear shrill voices squealing: 'Coo' and 'Cor Blimey, the rotten tykes,' and 'What horrid

71

little boys have been in our locker room?'

What nasty little minds! I ruminated. They're already blaming the boys. Soon there were prefects to-ing and fro-ing with stern-faced teachers. Obviously, this was not an amusing incident.

As the courtyard became increasingly crowded, a strange hush descended over the whole area. Everybody was talking in whispers. After all, vandalism on this scale was a rarity in such a well disciplined school. And I'm sure there was more than one person who reckoned that the damage may well have come from outside the orphanage.

Instinctively I knew that there was only one course of action for Ped and I. Whichever way we turned the outcome was going to be bad, but owning up was our only salvation. I think Ped realised this too, and although a touch reluctant at first, he required little persuasion.

'Come on Ped, for God's sake, hurry up, we've got to give ourselves up and tell Old Ruggs before anyone else gets to him first.'

We both realised that it did not require a lot of detective work before the finger of suspicion pointed straight at us. Ped just grunted in agreement. His face had taken on that typical blank expression which meant that I would have to do the talking and he would accept his fate.

We met the Head just coming out of his study. Luckily for us, it was as clear as day that the demise of the wellingtons had not yet reached his ears.

'Hello boys, haven't you seen enough of me today?' he joked. 'Ha ha, well, what can I do for you?'

Ruggs never managed another word for the next five minutes as I confessed to our crime and told him how stupid and sorry we were, and what dashed bad luck it was for him to have two such terrible boys bothering him.

As I went on . . . and on . . . talking, I watched his face change from serene . . . to thoughtful . . . to dismay . . . to disbelief to . . . complete fury. I was quick to emphasise the fact that we had come to confess of our own free will, and were ready to take our punishment, and also to pay for new wellies with our pocket money.

I think that was the moment we saved our skins. He could now approach any committee and justify himself for not expelling us. After all, two of his boys with tears welling in their eyes, boys who knew they had been very bad, had come to him on their own accord and begged forgiveness.

Even so, old Ruggs was still very angry and

this time we were caned good and proper. A beating which almost matched the beating that Roy and his mates suffered for the fire bucket episode.

We also did not receive any pocket money for a very long time.

5

Holiday and War

Before World War Two, West Wittering was a wild and lovely spot, tailor-made for any youngster with an adventurous spirit. Our holiday home was located approximately midway between Selsey Bill and Portsmouth, as near to the sea on the south coast as one could wish. This then was also the venue for my first ever orphanage vacation.

Unable to contain myself, I literally bubbled over with excitement on arrival at our bungalow. Only it was not exactly a bungalow.

Mr Gibb, one of our junior masters, said a bungalow would have been far too expensive for the likes of us. So we stayed in converted railway carriages, and they were jolly good. There was one carriage for the big boys, one for the big girls and one for the tykes, which was the nickname for little ones like us.

The following morning, all nine girls and boys of our carriage sat down for breakfast with our teachers, Mr. Hacket and Miss Clarke. This was the first time I had the dubious privilege of sitting down at the same table with girls. Although I was very shy at first, secretly I liked the change. I would never admit this to anyone, of course.

'Hugo, calm yourself down please, and don't gobble up your food so quickly,' I was told. 'My goodness me, ever since we arrived you have resembled a little Jack rabbit bobbing up and down all over the place. Perhaps you have not had enough to eat. How would you like another boiled egg?'

'Cor, yes please, Sir, I'm starving,' I said.

Back in my seat and bursting with glee, I firmly tapped the top of the egg with my teaspoon, and beheld an empty shell. My transformation was instant. From a look of sheer delight, my face registered misery, disappointment and frustration. I was still hungry.

Oh well, I thought, at least the ice for this holiday was broken. Everybody laughed their heads off, especially a little girl named Brenda on whom I'd played the same trick five minutes earlier.

'Hugo,' Mr. Hacket continued, smiling triumphantly. 'The biter has been bit, a phrase you will do well to remember, my son. Now children, off you go and play on the beach, but remember there is to be no swimming until Miss Clarke comes and assesses your ability in the aquatic arts. That's two 'remembers' for you this morning Hugo, is it not?'

'Yes Sir, thank you, Sir.'

Alec and I needed no encouragement. Alec was a good-looking, compact little fellow even smaller than me. Tough, daring, yet gentle. In all the years I knew him I cannot recall him moaning or uttering an unkind word about anybody. Although nearly two years younger than myself, we always enjoyed each other's company. Indeed, as a result of this holiday, we developed a solid friendship that lasted many years.

We headed pell-mell for the beach, soon outstripping the others.

'Where's the sea, where's the sea?' Alec cried out, for in all directions the beach appeared endless.

First, we encountered the soft rolling dunes, marked with clumps of spiky green grasses which eventually gave way to flatter but still soft dry sand, devoid of any foliage. As we drew nearer to the water's edge, the sands rippled and hardened, feeling slightly uncomfortable under our bare feet.

'Look, Alec,' I said, pointing to a derelict hulk way in the distance. 'Let's wade out and explore.'

'Gosh, it's a long way out,' he replied,

unsure about my idea.

Soon we reached the wreck and easily clambered aboard, though we were still only knee-deep in water. To a grown-up, the old relic was probably of no consequence. The powerful off-shore winds and waves had battered the poor thing into a remnant. But there was enough of the boat left for us to be interested, the wind, the waves and everything else being of minor importance to us for the time being.

'Bergie, quick, come and see these queer fish.'

I could tell by his voice that Alec was excited. I ran over to the seaward side.

'Crikey, we're being invaded by jellyfish, look there's hundreds and hundreds of them.'

'Let's catch one.'

'No fear Alk, they may be poisonous. Miss Clarke said we were to avoid jellyfish because they have a frightful sting.'

Neither of us had ever seen jellyfish before, at least not in the flesh, although those transparent blobs did not look like flesh to me. They reminded me of gigantic masses of frogs spawn that had been separated by the force and power of the sea. I could just imagine the giants depicted in fairy tales and mythological stories, eating them as if they were tapioca pudding. For about five minutes we stared in fascination at these creatures of the sea.

'Do you know Alk, I think they've come here all the way from Portugal and drifted in with the tide, at least I think that's what Miss Clarke said they do. She said there's one called the Portuguese Man o' War or something like that, and it's so poisonous it can kill a man.'

'Well we're safe as long as they don't climb aboard, and they are not likely to do that without legs.'

'That's true, Alec, but aren't they weird?' I never mentioned the dangling stringy bits that might have been capable of clambering over the side of the boat and stinging us something horrid.

Alec was peering over the edge of our wreck, making sure his hands were well away from these strange floating blobs of life.

'Where is Portugal anyway?' he chirped.

I thought hard for a moment, and remembered a picture of Christopher Columbus gazing out to sea as a young boy, in the company of an old sailor.

'It has a coast like ours' I replied, 'only it's a lot warmer, cos Portugal is a lot further south than we are.'

After searching my memory further, I was able to show off another little gem of my geographical wisdom. 'Its on the edge of Europe, and there is miles and miles of ocean until you reach America. I suppose the jellyfish come up here in the summer and go back home when they get too cold.'

'Yeah I s'pose you must be right. Blinking heck! Oh God! Bergie, the front end of the boat is under water.'

'Blimey, the darn tide's coming in.'

All thoughts of jellyfish instantly vanished from our minds. I knew I mustn't panic. Alec had yet to learn to swim.

'Help help!', we shouted and waved our hands for all we were worth. I had never been so frightened as the two of us stood shivering with cold and fear, while the unforgiving waters swirled and eddied ever-higher up our bodies. One or two jellyfish passed by too close for comfort, their transparent bodies floating flibberty jibberty on the swell. We were in big trouble.

Then suddenly we saw our teacher Miss Clarke heading toward us, pushing an air bed through the waves.

It was a silent rescue. No tears. No telling off. All three of us were so relieved that speech was unnecessary. And as the wreck disappeared under the waves so too did any further reference to the frightening incident we had just experienced.

★ ★ ★

A few days later, Alec and I were scampering along the cliff top, hoping we would eventually come across the ancient abandoned church we had heard about. Apparently, its belfry was still reasonably intact. What's more, this time-worn place of worship was said be inhabited by horrifying bats exhibiting vampire-like tendencies.

While strolling along, I also noticed the subtle changes in the landscape. The salty winds sweeping in from the sea had sucked up any moisture and the hot August sun had created a dry, seemingly barren coast line. The vegetation had become sparse and stunted.

As we continued along this coastline, we noticed something else was different too. Different even from when we had first arrived. All at once, I realised what had changed. Here and there interspersed amongst the sparse plant life were bundles of barbed wire, strategically dropped into place.

Naturally, Alec and I were utterly unaware of the Third Reich which was already on its inexorable march through Europe. Nor did we understand the rumbling clouds of war that were gathering. Nor were we aware that Great Britain would soon become involved.

Occasionally, we heard grown-ups speaking quietly among themselves about a man named Hitler. Seeing all this barbed wire, however, disturbed me because it seemed so alien to the peaceful surroundings.

'It's a funny thing, Bergie, but I wonder why we weren't punished for going out to that wreck the other day?'

Alec's voice brought me back from my daydream.

'Yeah, it was a bit strange, I guess sometimes grown-ups are difficult to understand. It's a bit like when I was late for prep. Oh! Of course you weren't with us then. I tell you what Alec, if you promise not to laugh and keep it to yourself, I'll tell you about another time I never got punished.'

'I won't tell, Bergie, honest I won't.'

'Right, it was a day similar to this one, sort of peaceful and quiet, apart from the noise we were making,' I began. 'A group of us were heading back to the locker-rooms to clean up before prep, when one of the prefects turned round and asked John to nip down to the village for him. Well, as you know, our John is hardly the chap to nip anywhere. He's not really built for nipping. Poor John, he started fretting, and complained that he could never make it there and back in time for prep. The rotten prefect insisted though, gave him a

82

threepenny joey and told him to get a penneth of bent nails and to keep the change.'

'Poor old John, did he fall for it?'

'Yeah, he certainly did, but so did I. That rotten sod of a prefect knew that John would be unable to get back in time. Besides, I heard him saying to Bob that it's about time the new boy was tested. 'I'll go,' I said, and snatched the threepenny bit and headed off as fast as I could.'

Alec started chuckling at this point.

'Sorry, Bergie I'm not laughing at you, but you . . . Oh never mind, carry on.'

'That's okay, Alec, but that's not the whole story. I needed the money and just ran off without even thinking about it. I hadn't seen any money for ages and it seemed like an easy way of earning tuppence. Besides, I felt a bit sorry for John, especially as he was new. Anyway, I was late for prep but not by much. Bomber Howells was our form teacher that week, so you can imagine how timidly I entered the classroom.'

'Oh Gawd, what did he say?'

'I'll tell you,' I said, suddenly imitating Bomber Howells: 'Why are you late Hugo? Hell's bells, you scruffy little urchin.' (I hadn't had time to clean up you see Alk.)

'Where have you been Master Bergström?'

I really thought I was in trouble. I explained to him that I had been sent to buy some bent nails in the village and that I ran all the way there and back as fast as I could.

'Alas, not quick enough Hugo. And tell me, what did the shopkeeper say? . . . No don't bother, I know what he said. Do you want me to tell you what he told you?'

I tell you Alk, I saw a bit of a smile on his face, but I thought he would be really angry. I asked him how he could possibly know what the shopkeeper said.'

'Go on, Bergie, what did he say?' Alec butted in again, hardly able to contain himself.

'Well, Bomber stood up and boomed out for all the class to hear:

'The shopkeeper told you that he'd sold out of bent nails, but would a pennyworth of straight hooks do instead'!'

By now Alec was rolling around with laughter.

'You promised not to laugh, Alk', I said in a mock hurt tone.

'I know Bergie, but . . . '

'Every one else was laughing too, I tell you. Except myself and John. John wasn't laughing, because he was blinking well missing. That prefect was a real rotter. He insisted that John should go and see what the skyline looked like and report back to describe it to him.'

'Blimey, Bergie, what was the name of this rotten prefect'

'That's just what Bomber asked me. You see he still hadn't quite finished with me. I thought, he seems to know everything else, its a wonder he doesn't know the chap's name either. I didn't tell him of course, I just made some sort of excuse like 'I sort of volunteered Sir.' Then Bomber looked straight at me for a long moment and then told me to go and sit down. Anyway, I never did get the cane for being late. I guess you never can tell with grown-ups.'

By now the terrain had become even more rugged. The few trees in our vicinity were leaning inland, pointing all their pokey branches away from the sea. The only movement was the swaying of branches in the gentle breeze. The only sound was the gentle swishing of the sea, now and again interrupted by the shrill cry of lone seagull. Way up in the heavens, the blazing sun shone down through a cloudless sky. There was no sign of habitation, until we rounded a bend and saw a man and woman arguing.

As we scurried by, Alec whispered: 'Cor, look, he's hitting her.'

When I witnessed the man slapping the

poor woman again on the face, I shouted: 'Leave her alone you rotten sod!'

He turned and then started walking purposefully towards us. From his angry face, it was plain he wasn't coming over just to say hello. We needed no further encouragement to put distance between ourselves and his horrible presence.

Finally, we reached the summit of the cliff path and not more than two hundred yards away, the old abandoned belfry stood out like a lone sentinel. In the background, a ceaseless multitude of white horses were rolling in with the advancing tide. The scene was so serene, it could have been created from an artist's paintbrush.

Scampering down to our goal we entered a huge hole where once, no doubt, an oaken door had filled the gap. Inside, the rickety stairways were so vertical that we wondered how we were going to get to the top. Carefully, we climbed up the three angled ladders, strategically placed to enable us to reach the platform where the bell was once housed.

The bell was no longer there and if there were ever bats in this belfry, we saw no sign of them. Indeed, what was left of this tower gave refuge only to birds, many of which were squawking in protest against our invasion of their innermost sanctuary.

As the last of the birds temporarily flew away, we became aware of the silence. Even the incoming tide was barely audible. Suddenly, we experienced utter stillness and quiet combined with a vast empty space. A feeling of nothingness engulfed us uninterrupted by the flat calm ocean, which stretched unblemished to the hazy horizon. Moments like this never last, but the memory of it is still with me today.

Suddenly an excited chattering of young voices broke the serenity.

'Where's all that noise coming from?' Alec asked.

'Crumbs, there are some kids coming this way.' I replied. 'I think they're ours, and Miss Clarke is with them. Come on, let's go and meet them, they are bound to be looking for us. I told Brenda at breakfast that we were going to search for the old belfry.'

* * *

'War! War! The Germans are coming,' Trevor shouted, and at the same time he skipped down the hill in his excitement to be the first to impart the important news to us. Trev was the youngest in our group, far too young to have come with Alec and I on our adventure. After all, I was ten and Alec was nine.

I must have had a puzzled expression on my face because Miss Clarke said: 'We are all going back to the bungalow for the time being Hugo. There are things that need to be discussed concerning the immediate future.'

Naturally, we assumed that our holiday was about to be cut short. And Miss Clarke, reading the disappointment on our faces added: 'But I expect Mr. Hacket will try and get permission to see if we can remain a bit longer.'

The late afternoon was still warm, and the air was quiet and sultry, despite the tide being nearly full. An aura of tranquillity enveloped me as we returned to the top of the cliff path. I turned round and took one last look at the old belfry standing all alone with the sea at its back. I took a mental snapshot of the scene. I hope the Germans leave our belfry alone, I thought.

'Come on, Hugo, you don't want to miss your tea.'

I turned round and faced Miss Clarke.

'No, Miss, I don't. Do you think the Germans will come from the sea? There's an awful lot of barbed wire all over the place, isn't there? Is Hitler a very bad man. Miss Clarke?'

'Yes, Hugo, he is, but we will deal with him by and by. Now stop being such a chatterbox

88

and catch up with the others.'

'Yes, Miss Clarke.'

Miss Clarke was true to her word, we did have more time at West Wittering. In fact, we were to have the rest of August and some of September too.

*   *   *

Usually Ped went to his Gran's for the summer vacation, but because of his Gran's death, the authorities decided he would come to Wittering this year. Unfortunately he was rushed to hospital for an ear operation. Because of this untimely intervention, he joined us later, and though the older boys and girls groaned and moaned when they heard that the terrible twins were back together again, they had to agree we added spice to their lives.

Day after day, the sun blazed on its solitary way across cloudless skies.

One morning there was more activity than usual coming from the big boys carriage.

'Come on Ped, let's see what's happening,' I said with my usual early morning enthusiasm. We soon discovered they were going to Winkle Bay for the day.

'Can we come with you?' Ped shouted hopefully through their open window.

'Nope, its too far for you two tykes,' replied Arnie in an authoritative tone, wondering whether he had the backing of the others.

'No, it's not, and anyhow, we'll jolly well follow you, if you don't let us come!' Ped insisted.

'Let the lads go with you Arnold,' Mister Gibb interrupted. 'If they are as tough as their reputation, the three mile walk each way won't hurt them.'

Good old Mr. Gibb. I'd never seen him before our holiday, and after the vacation finished, I never saw him again. Later I could only assume he went off to war. He was certainly capable of looking after a bunch of unruly orphans, and he was very popular with the older chaps, for whom he was responsible. The older girls were under the matronage of Mrs. Surridge, our sewing mistress, while we Tykes remained under the kindly wings of Mr. Hackett and Miss Clarke.

★ ★ ★

Winkle Bay was a truly splendid experience. Ped and I soon forgot our tired legs, and the Lord only knows how many raw winkles we ate. The oohs and aahs and discoveries in all the rock pools, nooks and crannies were far too numerous to count.

Hours later, on the way back, the big chaps wanted to go snooping in the village shops. But Ped and I, not having any money, decided to carry on home to our train.

We still had a fair distance to walk, when Ped broke the silence by saying in a slightly tired voice: 'I spent all my pocket money the first day I arrived'.

'Yeah, me too,' I said. 'Miss Clarke said that as we are having an extended holiday, we will get some extra pocket money next week. I bet the others don't have two ha'pennies to rub together either . . . except Granville, of course. He always seems to have money.'

After a moment or two, Ped asked 'What do they want to bother with the shops for then?'

'Dunno really. Perhaps they are going pinchiosis.'

'Pinchiosis, what's that?' Ped said with increasing interest.

'You know, when a couple of chaps go into a shop, one of them buys a farthing worth of chews or something, and while the shop-keeper's not looking, the other bloke grabs something.'

'But that's stealing!'

'That's right. I certainly won't do it again. While you were in hospital, Alec and I pinched a few things from Morrisons. At the time we saw no harm in it. It was great fun swiping stuff from under his nose. In no time at all, we had collected half a dozen golf balls and a few pencils and rubbers. Even an H-type fishing line. Alec hid the lot under his bed in a big biscuit tin.'

'Crikey, my Gran would have been upset if . . . '

Poor old Ped, I thought, he still misses his Gran.

'Yeah, but at first, I didn't think it was stealing. Just sort of borrowing . . . without permission. We weren't going to keep the stuff. We were going to sneak it back at the end of the holiday. I'm glad we got caught though, it taught us a lesson. I shan't ever go pinchiosis again. Alec heard the big boys talking about it and that gave us the idea I s'pose.'

'What happened after you were found out?' Ped's curiosity was now fully aroused.

'Well Ped, you mustn't mention this to a soul. I'm only telling you 'cos you and Alec are my best friends.'

I paused to collect my thoughts. 'Well it was the cleaning woman who comes in once a week. While sweeping under the bed, she noticed the biscuit tin, and she could not resist poking her nose under the lid. Cor blimey, from the way she called us all a lot of rotten thieves and stormed off after Mr. Hacket, you'd have thought we'd pinched the Crown Jewels. Anyway, Alec and I ran off into the sand dunes to hide from the police. We were sure they would come after us. But we were wrong. So after what seemed ages and ages, back we went to face the music.

'Blinking heck! Were you caned?'

'Nope. It was much worse than that. Mr. Hacket gave us a terrible ticking off. I still can't forget the way he looked at me saying: 'Hugo, how on earth could you do such a bad thing.' I felt ever so bad and sorry. I even told him I deserved the cane. He said: 'No Hugo. You're not going to get off that easily. Do you realise that not too many years ago, you could have been shipped off in chains to Australia and branded as convicts for stealing?'

'I tell you, Ped, Alec and I were close to tears before he finished speaking to us. Then came a knock on the door and a Bobby strode in. Ever-so tall he was. He had to stoop down to get through the entrance. And when he stood up straight, his helmet almost touched the ceiling. Oh crumbs, I thought. We're in real trouble. After a few words with the policeman, Mr Hacket turned to us and told us that we were to go with the policeman.'

'Crikey, were you scared?'

'Not half, we really believed we were going to prison. It certainly was a horrid shock.'

'Well, what happened next?' asked Ped impatiently, hardly able to contain himself.

'He took us to the shop. The Bobby didn't say much. Nor did we, come to think of it. But after confessing to the shopkeeper and saying how sorry we were, the policeman asked Mr. Morrison if he wanted us locked up in prison with the other criminals. Mr Morrison put his hand to his chin for what seemed ages and then said 'no, not this time', but if we ever even looked like stealing again, he would throw the book at us. Which blinking book he meant, I don't know, but I bet it would have been a big one! I haven't been in the shop since, nor will I. There is one more thing for certain too. I will never go pinchiosis again.'

Soon our unforgettable vacation drew to a close. I still remember this holiday vividly, for it was the first proper long summer holiday by the seaside I had ever experienced.

6

Christmas, 1939

The onset of winter in 1939 began earlier than usual. The cold weather from the East quickly gained an icy foothold throughout the land. Already the early mornings of late November were receiving unwelcome attention from Jack Frost. The dreaded itchy jersey was a necessary garment out of doors. The shorts we wore the whole year round but our long socks, held up with elastic garters, were sufficient to keep us warm.

It was on one such crisp and frosty morn as I was pondering how apt the name 'Silverlands' was that my thoughts were abruptly interrupted.

'Come here, boy,' said the gruff voice of Old Irvy. Old Irvy was one of the nicer nicknames we labelled him with. Mr Irving was one of the new teachers who joined us when our orphanage moved from Langley Hall to Silverlands. I liked him almost as much as Mr. Simpson, but I learnt from our first encounter to be wary of his walking stick.

★　★　★

Oh dear, I thought, what does Old Big Bum want. I knew better than to pretend not to hear. Even a stone deaf person could hear his voice. We had also learned not to take liberties with this teacher even though he was generally considered a good bloke as teachers go.

'Yes Sir,' I said, before I had even turned round. I then started walking towards him, stopping before I got too close to his big stick.

'Yes Sir,' I repeated, while stealing a quick glance into his eyes, in an attempt to assess his mood.

Old Irvy was a large hefty man. Sometime in the past he had contracted polio or something leaving him with a gammy leg. The result was that he needed a stick to help him walk.

I kept a wary eye on his leg support, for I knew from experience he was capable of handling it in a variety of ways and with plenty of dexterity. He reminded me of a great big grizzly bear — reasonably loveable, but to be treated with the utmost respect.

Reflecting on days gone by, the innocent accuracy with which young children can analyse grown-ups never ceases to amaze me.

'Well, son, I haven't seen you in the tuck shop queue lately,' he said, bending a little nearer to me. 'Why's that?'

A considered response was required here, I thought. He must have known about my pocket money officially being stopped, but did he know they forgot to carry it through? Oh well, I'd best tell the truth, I thought.

'I'm saving up for Christmas, sir. But it ain't half difficult.'

'You mean, 'it is very difficult', not 'it ain't half difficult', Hugo.'

I could see by the quizzical look on his face that my answer to his question had puzzled him.

In theory, we were allowed twopence a week pocket money, but by the end of the average week I was lucky to end up with a farthing. In those days, a farthing was the most common coin in my pocket. One had to be the Archangel Gabriel himself to qualify for the full amount.

However, for the past three weeks, I had been making a special effort and had managed to save fourpence. Obviously, Mr. Irving had come to the conclusion that I was stony broke because of being extra naughty.

'Explain yourself, boy,' he growled, stretching up to his full height so that I had to crane my neck to see his face. As this was uncomfortable, I spoke to his ample stomach instead.

'I'm going to buy myself a smashing Christmas present and post it to myself, sir. I've seen some of the other boys opening their parcels with tons of tuck inside, but I'm going to have soldiers.'

Once again I tilted my face upwards to read whatever I could in his face. I had learned early in life that grown-ups were often worse than kids at hiding their feelings. In his face, I saw sadness and compassion.

'Report to me tomorrow morning after assembly Hugo, as I have an errand for you. Now be off with you, and do not be late for prep or else your next week's pocket money will be in jeopardy.'

★   ★   ★

The very next morning I knocked on old Irvy's door thinking that he might give me a penny for the errand whatever it was.

'Come in, Hugo. I see you have remembered our appointment,' he said, stifling a yawn. 'I want you to go to the village Post Office, buy a stamp and post this letter, and here is an extra penny for your trouble.'

'Thank you, sir, I'll go right away,' I said, grabbing the money quickly, but as graciously as possible. Trying not to appear rude, I hurried off before he had time to change his mind about the penny.

It wasn't too far to the Post Office so I was able to run all the way. I didn't even pause to see if the frogs were hopping about in the stream that meandered alongside the lane — it was probably a bit late in the year anyway. I remember thinking how Alec took one of these frogs out of the stream, and plonked it in Monty's desk drawer. Boy, was she mad.

On reaching the Post Office I clambered up the side of the pillar box, shoved the letter through the opening, then popped into the shop and bought the stamp. It was not until I was halfway back to Silverlands that it suddenly dawned on me that all was not well.

Oh Crikey! I thought. I've still got the blasted stamp. What the heck can I do now? I know, I'll just say nothing. No no, that's no good. He's bound to find out and then he'll think I've cheated him out of another penny. Old Irvy would be furious. Besides I don't steal anymore. I would have to tell him damn it. Any other course of action was completely out of the question.

★　★　★

99

The orphanage was a good educator in more ways than one. Among other things, I learned that when in trouble, take the bull by the horns and face up to your problems.

Summoning up the most crest-fallen face I could manage, I sheepishly reported back to Mr. Irving. stammering my way through the necessary excuses.

'You stupid boy,' he thundered. 'What a moronic thing to do.'

'Excuse me, sir, what does moronic mean?'

'Get out, get out,' he said half raising himself from his chair with the aid of his stick. Still clutching the penny, I was gone in a jiffy.

The first heavy snowfall of the year was early. And on this particular Winter's morn, I looked out the dormitory window in amazement. The lawns and fields had merged into a single virgin white carpet stretching right up to the woodland edge where all the trees were dressed in dazzling white, save for a splash of green where the falling snow flakes had been unable to gain a foothold.

For the first time in my life, the splendour of Mother Nature held me spellbound and cried out to me: Come and see what I have to offer!

After a hurried breakfast, I grabbed my cap and blazer and slipped unnoticed into the forest without telling a soul.

Today I wanted to be alone. There were two or three hundred acres at my disposal to roam in. I paused and listened. For one golden moment, it was so quiet I could hear the silence. I then became aware of all sorts of forest noise and realised how abundant and varied was the woodland life, despite the inhospitable cold weather.

Later I came across two squirrels dashing here and there. I spoke to them out loud. 'Has the winter caught you by surprise?' I asked. 'You should be gathering some food, or else later you may both go hungry, especially if the snows lay deep.'

They scurried away, startled perhaps by my voice.

I was heading in the general direction of Big Ben. Big Ben was the name we had given to our toboggan run. Not that we had toboggans to zoom down the hill on. We used old chair-backs which we converted into home-made sleighs. Poor Fitz was working on one of these when he had his terrible accident. There was only room for one sleigh at a time to have a go, so to make things exciting, we devised a method of timing the runs. Our method was pretty basic. The chief timer at the top of the mini Cresta run would shout 'GO', whereupon the participant would hurtle himself and the home-made contraption down the slope, and the chief timer would start timing. The chief timer may have owned or borrowed a watch. But if not, he would simply start counting to himself, 'ONE AND TWO AND THREE AND . . . ' and so on.

The assistant timer, waiting at the bottom of the run by the finishing line, would holler 'FINISHED' when the participant crossed the line, whereupon the chief timer on hearing this would note the amount of seconds it had taken. We spent many happy hours occupying ourselves in this fashion . . . apart from the times when we crashed and occasionally hurt ourselves.

How strange I thought, this snow seems very deep here, when suddenly without any warning, I fell through a hole.

I had been walking on top of some rhododendron bushes where the drifting snow had piled up, and the weight of my body was just enough to break through. Luckily, I only dropped a few feet onto the forest floor.

To my amazement, I found myself in a tunnel, a tunnel created by nature, all of two hundred yards long. The sides were thick and matted and virtually impenetrable. As if by design and over many seasons, Mother

Nature had added layer upon layer of Rhododendron growth, and woven it all magically together to form a roof. The added blanket of snow finished the job off, keeping the passage in semi-darkness. Although a little shaken I wasn't at all frightened. In fact I felt a little elated. 'Cor', I thought, 'I've found a secret passage. Wait until I tell my friends. I mustn't tell anybody else though, we must keep this place a secret.'

Bent double, I made my way to one end where I had to lay down and force an opening big enough to squirm through into the fresh air and daylight. Brushing the snow off my clothing, I noticed that I had grazed my knee to the extent that blood had trickled down onto my sock. I remember thinking how strange it was that it didn't hurt until I'd noticed the blood.

It seemed like hours before I finally broke out of the woods and came by the churchyard in the village of Lyne. A weather-beaten old man was digging a new hole among the gravestones. Despite the cold, his shirt sleeves were rolled up to his elbows revealing tree-trunk like forearms. His coat was draped over a nearby gravestone.

'Good morning, young sir,' he said. 'I can see by your blazer that you are from the orphanage.'

'That's right, mister. I've been walking in the woods for a long time, but I sort of knew my way out here. I found a secret tunnel, but I don't think I will tell anyone, 'cos then it stops being a secret. I was hoping to see a red squirrel, 'cos I was really quiet, but all I managed to find were two grey ones.'

'Yes,' the man replied, 'there are one or two red squirrels left in these woods, but I daresay they will be gone before you're much older. When I was your age, it was the grey squirrel that was a rarity.'

'We have some grey squirrels as pets at Silverlands,' I told him. 'Well, not me exactly, but Len and Granville do. They've trained them ever so good, they have. D'you know what? When Gran or Len calls them, the squirrels rush down from the tree. They then pick them up and throw them back up into the tree only to rush back down again. After a few times they get some food. It's hard to believe but it's the honest truth. They keep them in a big cage.'

Leaning towards the grave digger, I continued: 'See the hole in my cap? That's where the lid of the cage fell on my head, and a nail sticking out went through the cap into my head. Didn't hurt much though, I bet the cap helped me a bit.'

'That's very interesting,' said the polite

gravedigger, leaning heavily on his spade.

'I know why you're digging that hole. Somebody has died, haven't they? And you're going to bury the dead person. It must be awful to go down there.'

'Well, son, if you go to church here every Sunday and listen to what the vicar says, you'll soon realise that there's a part of you that lives forever and does not go down there. And that's the part that matters.'

'My mum died ages ago. They say I screamed and screamed when they pulled me out of her arms. I don't remember 'cos I was only two.'

The gravedigger started shovelling again and we both fell silent for a while, him digging and me watching. Then he leaned on his spade once more before climbing out of his hole and reaching for his coat.

'Never mind, son, what with the war and all, I dare say there'll be many more like you before we're through. Look, here's a penny. Go get yourself a cake or something, and run on home before you catch your death.'

'Cor, thanks mister, it's been awful nice meeting you. My name's Hugo but all the kids call me Bergie 'cos of my last name, being Bergström. That's Swedish, you know. My grandpa was from a place called Karlskrona. He was in the navy. Then he came to England and worked on a farm. I wish I was on a farm. Silverlands is a nice place but some of the time I am unhappy. I'm getting cold, mister. Thanks for chatting with me . . . and for the penny, of course.'

★ ★ ★

Christmas was looming ever nearer and I was looking forward to it even more this year. Being rich made a great deal of difference. I had managed to save ninepence and, boy oh boy, it was a great strain during those long weeks trying to be a goodie-goodie. But now I could be normal again. Ped and I were going out this very afternoon to buy my soldiers.

I said: 'Let's go and fetch our blazers and clear off before some clever dick nosey parker gives us a job.'

As soon as I put the blazer on, I knew the money was gone. My pocket just didn't jangle any more. Half sobbing and half choking with rage and feeling very sorry for myself, I gave way to my feelings and cried out.

'Crikey, it took me ages and ages to save that up. I had to go without tuck and everything. What rotten sod would steal my ninepence?' I sobbed.

Ped just looked at me, pity showing in his face. He didn't know how to console me.

Tears streaming down my face, I ran across and out of the cobbled courtyard to the huge coal bunker.

When upset, this was the place I often headed for to avoid contact with others. It was bad enough that Ped had seen me start crying. After about five minutes moping, swearing and hurling stones at the perfectly innocent coal bunker, it dawned on me that the money may have not been stolen, but had just fallen out of my pocket while playing. And that meant findums keepums.

Oh well, I reasoned, at least I don't have to put up with being too good any more, and I damn well won't cry over a few soldiers, besides I will still get my sock filled up Christmas morning, even though a lump of coal will fill half of it.

By now, dependable old Ped had rejoined me. He knew how much it hurt, and said: 'Come on Bergie, let's go to the flicks. Convict 99 is on at the flea pit in Addlestone. Will Hay is . . . '

Interrupting and with some enthusiasm seeping back into my day I agreed. 'Okay, you will have to lend me tuppence though.'

'I know that, I wouldn't have asked you if I didn't have enough money for both of us, would I?' he answered a little testily. 'I've got fourpence halfpenny and that means if we walk both ways we can have some farthing chews as well.'

Without further ado, off we went.

Arriving at the cinema queue, we looked for a likely candidate to take us in. This was a much safer way than sneaking in through the exit doors, and with fewer repercussions if you were caught. In no time at all, we latched on to a bloke who could pass for our guardian, and nonchalantly walked in with him. We both thought the film was great and well worth the effort of hoofing it there and back.

'Golly, I'm starving,' I said to Ped as we made our way back to Silverlands. 'Let's go and see what there is in the kitchen gardens.'

We had to be very careful raiding the gardens at Silverlands. The head gardener was none other than Bert Hazel. Both Mr. and Mrs. H were both very important members of staff in our school. And as the war intensified and lengthened, they became needed more and more.

Mr. And Mrs. H lived in a lovely bungalow on the edge of Silverlands. Little did I realise then that many years later, I was to be part of their family life.

Bert could run, and was equal to nearly every trick that we used in preventing detection. If you were silly enough to get caught, you could guarantee receiving a clip round the ear, as well as being reported. The thick ear came complete with the headmaster's blessing, plus whatever else he might add to the punishment. Raiding the kitchen gardens was a serious crime in the eyes of our authorities.

It had started to rain which was in our favour because there was less likelihood of anyone tramping about. We soon discovered that December was not a good time to go scrumping, but coming across some old beetroots that must have been in the ground for ages, we ate them. They tasted terrible and pretty soon our throats began to burn and hurt something horrible. We had no choice but to go and tell Sister what happened. Dear Sister was a brick, and did not report us. She said we had been punished pretty severely without any more troubles heaped upon us. I have never eaten old beetroot since.

'Wake up, Bergie, Happy Christmas.' It was 4 'o clock in the morning when Alec woke me up.

Christmas Day found us diving into our socks which were dangling at the end of our beds. Miraculously, my sock was full and over-flowing, and between the lumps of coal and all sorts of other oddments, a tangerine, some nuts and, wonder upon wonder, I spied a piece of chocolate. Boy, what a feast!

Without a care in the world we all trooped off to church in line, being very polite to our teachers, thinking quite rightly that our Christmas dinner may very well be at stake on the way we behaved.

Come dinner-time, as reverently as possible, we all filed into the spacious dining-room for our meal of the year, consisting of succulent turkey, garnished with sweet red cranberry jelly, roast potatoes, sprouts and other fresh produce from the kitchen gardens, despite the frequent raids the long-suffering vegetable patch had to endure during the growing season.

This was followed by flaming Christmas pudding, albeit unceremoniously plonked on our plates, but nevertheless very welcome, especially with the addition of lashings of custard.

But even yet the happy day was not over. As the clock struck three, the whole school was sitting in front of a huge Christmas tree and at its base gorgeously wrapped presents were piled high.

During the next hour or so, to my utter amazement, my name was called out. Yes, wonder of wonders, there was a parcel for me. With trembling hands I received my gift and walked quickly back to my place on the floor.

No Christmas present could have possibly meant more to anybody. I just sat there oblivious to one and all. After having torn away the wrapping, there lay revealed an old battered biscuit tin. I slowly lifted the lid, peered inside and very carefully pulled back the layer of cotton wool.

I was now gazing at some lead soldiers, the genuine article. The first soldier's head was broken off but I could mend that with a match stick. A Red Indian came out next. So what if his tomahawk was missing? I could easily pretend he had already thrown it at another soldier who was unable to stand anyway on account of a missing foot. Why there were even one or two new ones. I had had my Christmas present after all, and I was so happy, there were tears in my eyes. At that moment, I was a very happy boy indeed.

I never did find out, however, how this most precious gift had come about.

7

Last Days at Silverlands

In the first few months of 1940, the only reminder that our country was at war with Germany were the occasional times when I had the opportunity to scrounge a copy of the magazine 'War Illustrated' from one of the older boys.

One issue stands out vividly in my memory. Strangely enough, it depicted neither England nor Germany. The written article may well have been beyond my understanding, but one photograph in particular, I will never forget.

It was a picture of a few Finnish soldiers, clad all in white, each with a rifle slung over his shoulder. They were silently skiing over frozen wastes beyond the Russian lines in order to harass their enemy from behind. The picture touched a sorrowful chord in my imagination. I could not help but connect it with the biblical story of David fighting a lonely battle against Goliath.

But one late afternoon brought the hostilities a little nearer home. While playing outside with some other boys, we noticed a dog fight taking place directly over our heads.

The pilot of a Wellington bomber was engaged in deadly combat with some German fighter planes. The lumbering elephant of the sky was no match for the feline agility of the combined Messerschmidt assault. But the British pilot could really handle that old war plane, nevertheless. His final evasive cover was unbelievable. It seemed that the Wellington bomber climbed literally vertically, heading towards the clouds above and simply disappeared inside that blessed blanket of protection.

For the most part, however, during the spring of 1940, for us, it was almost as if World War II didn't exist.

Living at Silverlands was anything but a humdrum existence though, and life continued for all of us with the usual ups and downs of orphanage life. One glorious sunny day early in May, one particular event hit me hard.

'Bergie, Bergie, come quickly, Bomber wants to see us urgently.'

I looked up and saw Giff running towards me, unusually excited.

Peter Gifford was 18 months older than me, a real nice chap who I always got on well with. He was a completely different character from his brother Chris, who was my age.

Although the two brothers were not at Langley, their arrival at Silverlands had coincided with my return from West Wittering.

'Okay, I'm coming, I hope to blazes I'm not in trouble 'cos you don't 'alf sound alarming.'

'No, its nothing like that, we've been picked for the First Eleven.'

'For crying out loud, Giff, you must be kidding. I'm not old enough.'

'Well, Bomber thinks you are. Come on, we'd better not keep everybody waiting.'

Slightly dazed and a little breathless, we arrived at Bomber's quarters.

'Hello boys,' he said. 'I expect Peter has told you, Hugo, that you're both playing cricket for your school this afternoon.'

'Yes sir, thank you, sir,' I said, still in shock.

'No need to thank me, my boy. I have been watching you both, and indeed the two of you have shown that you have a natural talent for the game, and your enthusiasm knows no bounds. Yes, without doubt, you deserve the chance.'

To my surprise, Mr. Howells then warmly shook my hand, which was completely lost in his great mitt. 'Now off you go and don't be late for the team photograph at 11 o'clock.'

Still in a dream, I said to Giff: 'By crikey, I never expected to be chosen for the First Eleven this year. I wonder who's lost his place.'

'Don't worry about it, Bergie. Bomber knows what he's doing. Everybody says he's the best cricket coach the school has ever had. C'mon we must get changed and join the rest of the team out front for the photo.' (I still have this photograph, one of my most treasured mementos).

By midday, unable to contain myself any longer, I was flying down to the cricket field, far too early for the match, of course.

'Hello Gerry, what are you doing here so early?'

'I'm the official scorer today,' he replied. 'Foster's got a bad stomach, so I was roped in. It suits me though. I might get the chance to draw one or two sketches.'

If there was one thing Gerry had in abundance, it was his artistic ability with a pencil. At the moment though, he had other ideas.

'Tell you what, Bergie, let's play the roller horse game. It'll pass the time until the others arrive.'

★　★　★

In the 1920s, a great deal of farm work was accomplished with horses, and the ideal way of flattening a piece of land would be a horse-drawn roller. The roller attachment would normally hook onto the horse's pulling contraption by means of a large hook on each shaft. Of course, it would not do to place a farm horse between the shafts of this particular roller — the resulting horse manure may have been of benefit to the cricket square, but the hoof marks certainly would not have been. However, four or five boys on each shaft would provide sufficient horse-power, man-power or boy-power, depending on which way you look at it, to do a fine job of rolling the pitch.

'Yeah all right, but you'll have to show me how.'

Gerry immediately put on his authoritative air, and began spouting his verbal instructions. 'Well, it's like this. You stand between the shafts with a hand on each. Gosh, you can only just reach. Never mind, you'll manage. Now, as I lift the shafts up, you push yourself off the deck and up you go. Don't worry about being up in the air, your own body weight will bring you slowly back down.'

'Okay, I'll try anything once,' I said doubtfully.

As it happened, once was more than

enough. Neither of us considered the fact that I was a stone lighter, two years younger and several inches shorter than the kids who normally played this silly game.

I went up well enough, a little too quickly perhaps, but I didn't come down, at least not in the way that Gerry intended I should. My left hand slipped, and one of the iron hooks caught my wrist tearing a nasty gash in it. I fell to the ground after first colliding with the roller wheel on the way down.

Gerry filled me in later but, apparently, I was half unconscious, dizzy with pain, and my wrist was bleeding heavily.

But Gerry managed to stifle the flow of blood and with him holding my wrist tightly, we staggered all the way back to the Infirmary where good old Sister was able to take over.

By this time, I think I was out of shock. I remember looking up into Sister's face with pleading eyes and saying: 'Please Sister, make me better so I can play today.'

'Oh Hugo, I'll make you better, don't you worry your little head about that, but I am afraid you must face the fact that there will be no cricket for you today.'

★　★　★

That was the first time Sister ever saw me with tears in my eyes and she knew as well as I did the tears had no connection with my nasty injury. Poor old Gerry received a roasting from Sister, but thank goodness she didn't report him. In fact I learnt later that she congratulated him on the way he handled the emergency. I sincerely hope he fulfilled his boyhood ambition and one day became a doctor.

Sister saw to it that I stayed overnight in the sanatorium for observation, and spoiled me abominably. Being her only patient this night, she was able to devote a considerable amount of attention to me.

That evening, she came and sat down on my bed and we talked for ages. My arm throbbed a little, but otherwise I was very comfortable, apart from the annoyance of not being able to move my wrist. I had already recovered from the disappointment of missing the cricket match. I would get another chance.

★ ★ ★

Sister was new to the orphanage when we moved to Silverlands. A lovely woman who won me over with her concern and gentle manner. I even felt a little shy at first. All this attention was new to me . . . and I must admit, I liked it. She asked me a lot of questions, and she was really interested in listening to me talk.

'Where were you born, Hugo?'

I thought hard, vaguely remembering my brother Carol's version of my first years of existence.

'Well, I was nearly born on a train, Sister, but not quite. My mother told my father that I was coming in a hurry. My Dad pulled the communication cord to stop the train. My parents were then whisked away in a taxi to a hospital in North Kensington. That's where I was born. Poor Mum, she had a tough time. I had to have special milk, because she had tuberculosis caused by draughts on the stage. My brother had to tell me all this 'cos I was too young to remember. Carol said I've always been in a hurry ever since the day I was born. Am I talking to much Sister? Mister Simpson once told me that I must try hard to listen to what other people say, because that is the way to learn. He said you never learn anything while you're talking.'

'He is quite right Hugo, but their are times when talking is good for you, and I think this is one of those times,' Sister said. 'Besides, I am really interested in your story, and am learning from you! Have you any more of your ancient history locked up in that little head of yours?'

Only Mr Simpson had been able to open me up in the same way this lady did. Sister's silence encouraged me to continue.

'Mum and Dad were opera singers, but after I was born, my mother didn't sing any more. I know she was very happy though Sister, because I was healthy.

'I'll tell you what, though, and I've never told anybody this, but I know it's true. She prayed very hard for me and all her nun friends did as well. I was very lucky. The nuns looked after my mother and me for two years, and then she died. My brother said she caught double pneumonia and being so frail from tuberculosis, just passed away. My brother said I cried and cried for ages when she died, but I don't remember that. Before she died the Sisters converted her into a Catholic, whatever that means. Why is it you're a Sister, and yet you're not a nun?'

'Oh, I've never thought of that Hugo, could it be that we are all Sisters of Mercy? The nun's main job is to save souls with the aid of prayer, whereas we try to save lives with the aid of medicine.'

I paused to catch my breath.

'Then what happened, Hugo?'

'My grandmother came down from the

North to help my Dad look after both of us at a little place called Great Bentley. My grandmother was just about my first memory ever. I can see her now, dressed all in black from head to toe, a big tall frightening lady, standing with her hands behind her back in front of a fireplace. I wouldn't eat my carrots, so she made me sit on the floor in the corner for punishment. Maybe that's why she looked so tall. Carol said I didn't like her. My mother was a beautiful woman though. Sometimes when I secretly look at her photograph I feel like crying. Even though I cannot remember my Mum, there are times when I miss her a lot.'

'Oh Hugo, do you want to go on?'

'Yes I do, Sister. You're the first person I've ever spoken to like this, and it's making me feel good. Anyway, Grandma died when I was four. Poor Dad couldn't help us any more. He told my brother later that these were his two hardest and unhappiest years of his life. My brother and I were taken to a hostel in London and there we stayed until I was six, and that's when I first came to the Orphanage at Langley. I wish I could see my brother more, but he told me it was against the rules on account of him being older.'

There were tears in Sister's eyes as well as my own, and again she spoke quietly: 'Hugo, my dear, I am going to bring you a cup of cocoa and then you're to settle down for the night.'

Later, Sister came back with my drink, and stayed with me a little longer, but before going, bent down and kissed me on each eye. No one had ever shown me so much love before.

★ ★ ★

I remained in the school hospital wing for another two days, being thoroughly spoiled.

Then, after saying goodbye to Sister, I gingerly made my way out via the main entrance. Gerry and Alec were waiting for me.

'Hello, Bergie,' they said in unison.

Then Gerry said: 'I've got to buzz off in a moment, but I wanted to see how your wrist was.'

'You can't see much at the moment, Gerry, but I mentioned to Sister about you wanting to be a doctor, so she kindly told me all about how to mend a wound. She is ever so clever you know. Seeing as the doctor was not available, she had to do something quick. I had to squeeze as hard as I could above the wound while she cleaned it. The more it hurt, the more I squeezed so that was OK. Then she made what you call a butterfly. Afterwards she placed a padded split to prevent me moving my wrist. I didn't watch much, 'cos it made me feel all funny.

'When the doctor came and had a look, he told Sister she had made such a good job, there was no need for stitches. He said the torn flesh came together beautifully. To be honest he gave me the creeps. Only trouble is, I have to keep the splint on for a few more days.'

★　★　★

Alec felt it was his turn to say something. 'We've got the day off 'cos Noel Coward and Mary Pickford are coming. He's going to tell us all about the war or something. Miss Clarke said to me that future plans for us all will soon be revealed.'

'Yeah.' Gerry said, 'there's been rumours flying round that before long, we might all be moving again.

'Nah that can't be true. We haven't been here long.' I didn't like the idea of moving, especially if it interfered with my cricket. I had already missed two matches. Gerry continued speaking:

'All I know is that Noel Coward and Mary Pickford . . .'

'Who's Mary Pickford?' I butted in once more.

Gerry heaved a sigh as if to say 'shut up for a moment'. 'I've been told she is a famous and beautiful actress. They are coming to talk to all the grown-ups and prefects about the war, and how it will affect the school. Anyway I'm off now, can't hang about with you two tykes all day.'

'Okay, Gerry, and thanks for coming,' I said. 'Hey Alec, would you like to see my secret passage in the woods, it's ever so good.'

'Yeah, let's go,' he said as we cut off across the paddock.

'From the passage if we have time, we'll take a short cut through the woods to Chertsey and buy some stale cakes and biscuits (they weren't stale really, just what was left at the end of the day).'

'Good,' Alec replied, 'I'm starving.' Come to think of it, we always seemed to be hungry.

At that very moment, the miracle of Dunkirk was taking place.

The British Expeditionary Force was endeavouring to return home. An army heroic in its defeat was coming back reasonably intact, in order to lick its wounds and recuperate. Never before had so many boats sailed down the river Thames and out to sea to assist in the evacuation of our troops from the shores of France.

June 1940 was a month filled with rumours. What with talk of being invaded, and whisperings in the corridors that our school would have to move again, I was glad when things settled down and the war once again receded into the background.

Young as I was, the speeches we listened to on the radio by Winston Churchill were memorable. He told us that the 'Battle of Britain in the air' had been won.

The long summer days seemed endless, and I had at last had the opportunity to establish myself on the cricket team. Little did I realise however, that before the year was out, cricket would be displaced by baseball and my dreams of a cricketing career would be shattered.

★　★　★

My recollections of July and August of that year are so hazy, I can only assume that our life at Silverlands tinkled along quite smoothly while the war continued on.

But everything changed in September.

One day that month, every member of the school, young and old alike, were ushered into the Assembly room to hear the news that the 54 youngest of us were going to live in

America and that we were to be integrated into actors' and actresses' families in California.

These were indeed times of 'Great Expectations'.

Indeed, the leaves had barely begun to fall when early in October, the day of our departure to the New World arrived.

★ ★ ★

Shortly before then, something big had definitely been in the air. The whole school had been rounded up and assembled in the main hall. Conflicting rumours and whispered snatches of conversation could be heard all over the place.

The headmaster Mr. Green walked methodically up to the rostrum, past the grand piano where only weeks before the president of the Actors' Orphanage Noel Coward had entertained us.

'Boys and Girls', he commenced. 'The decision has been finalised. All those boys and girls under 15 are going to California and will be fostered with families for the duration of the war.'

My heart missed a beat. For me the news could not have been better. Perhaps my brother and I would be together at last.

'The preparations are at last complete. In three days time, you will all be taken to Euston station to begin your long journey. That is all the information I am allowed to divulge. Good luck and God bless you all.'

That was the last I ever saw of Mr Green, the headmaster whose claim to fame was that he never caned me which, in itself, was a minor miracle. Not that he needed to. Instead, he had that peculiar knack for making you feel so small when you were naughty, that the cane would have been a relief.

★　★　★

Our journey began at Euston in October 1940. We all boarded a train for Glasgow, complete with our gas masks and name tags. Coincidentally, the night of our arrival was also the night the German air-force chose to give the Clyde its biggest bashing so far. Yet despite the waves of planes bombing hell out of the shipyards near where we were staying, nobody seemed scared.

Originally, we were scheduled to sail out of Southampton, but the German submarines were having a field day in that area. But with a boat full of evacuees torpedoed and sunk there only a month earlier, the authorities decided we should sail from Scotland instead and take a more northerly route to America.

The following day, we boarded the Empress of Australia. One of the biggest in the world, ironically, this grand old liner was built by the Germans during the First World War for the Kaiser himself to go cruising round the planet after Germany had won the war.

Our immediate destination was Newfoundland.

The boat was crowded with Canadian soldiers, most of whom were wounded in the evacuation of Dunkirk. I remember one soldier in particular, a big handsome young man with straw-coloured hair and wild green eyes that darted all over the place. I stared, fascinated by his slightly dishevelled appearance. Then all of a sudden, those flashing green eyes locked with mine. It was a scary moment, far more frightening than the bombs of the night before though I don't know why.

★ ★ ★

Our sea journey was to begin at nightfall. As I was exploring the wonder of the ship with one or two other lads up on deck, we suddenly heard a commotion behind us. The big soldier with a shock of straw blonde hair was shouting and lashing out at other soldiers who managed to calm him down and take him below. As he passed me, his wild green eyes once again looked into mine. But this time I wasn't scared, I felt sorry for him. Then one of the soldiers came over to us and said: 'Don't worry lads, he's suffering from shell shock. He'll be okay after a couple of days in sick bay.'

With a strict blackout in force, there wasn't much to see on deck. So Ped and I contented ourselves by running up and down the main circular stairway which was thickly carpeted in a thick ruby red pile. Never before had I been in such luxurious surroundings, except maybe once when we kids were taken to the Lord Mayor's banquet.

'Crikey, Ped, I dunno about an Empress, but this boat must be fit for the King and Queen themselves.'

The next few days we moved down the Clyde towards the open sea, where final preparations were completed before we finally left the British Isles.

At long last, we were underway. Yet as we were continuing our exploration of all this floating opulence, I began to feel a little queasy. Our liner, having left the Lee of the Scottish Mainland was heading in a Westerly direction with a crew poised for whatever surprises the vast Atlantic had in store, the first of which was the growing size of the waves.

'Ped, I feel queer, I think I'm gonna be sick.'

'Blimey, Bergie, you look horrible. But cripes, don't throw up on these carpets or there's bound to be trouble. You go into the lav and then I'll fetch Monty.'

My first experience of seasickness came on suddenly. Unfortunately, it also lasted for six nights and seven days — the total time of our voyage to the North American continent.

On our second night at sea, we left the rest of the convoy behind. They were much too slow. A large ship like ours, moving at twelve knots, was too big a target. At twenty knots, the Empress zigzagged her way through the heavy swell. The skipper had ordered the erratic course for good reason. Somewhere out there in the murky depths while all the passengers were sleeping below decks, a 'Wolf Pack' had been reported. These were the new terrors of the deep: fine U-boats, with highly trained crews, ready and waiting to unleash their metal torpedo at a single command.

Then, suddenly the great boat shuddered from stem to stern as the gigantic screws churned the water into a milky froth and our Empress completed the sharpest turn she had ever endured. Sick as I was, however, I realised that the violent movement was serious.

Action stations alerted everybody on board. Bleary-eyed and apprehensive, fifty-three children were rudely awakened, struggled into their life jackets and lined up in a corridor.

The soldier with wild green eyes picked up the fifty-fourth and carried me from the sick bay up onto the boat deck.

In an ironic sort of way I was fortunate to have been so ill, because while all the other kids were lined up somewhere below, I was in the fresh air with a ringside seat and a personal bodyguard in case we had to abandon ship. My blonde-haired protector produced a blanket from God knows where, wrapped it round and held me still. I was ten years old yet this was only the second time that I felt really cared for. And to think I never even knew the name of this magnificent, shell-shocked, green-eyed Canadian soldier.

Once again, the ship shuddered as it completed another evasive lurch to starboard, and a good job it did.

Wide-eyed I gazed in awe and wonder, for out there in those sinister cold waters, gleaming with an iridescent light that penetrated the dark blanket of night, a silvery ghostly metal fish of destruction glided harmlessly by, not more than twenty five yards away.

Our skipper surely knew his business. Twenty-four hours earlier, he left the convoy and, relying on his ship's superior speed and radar, had the courage to go it alone. It was the right move because, in the end, he only had one torpedo to contend with. I also learned later that the convoy was decimated to such an extent that a large liner like ours would not have stood a chance. In those early days of the war, the U-boats played havoc not only with our Royal Navy, but with the Merchant Navy as well.

PART II – USA

PART II - USA

8

Confrontations

It was half way through October 1940 when we finally arrived in Halifax, Canada.

The journey from Nova Scotia to Montreal was spectacular. Hour after hour, all day and all night clickety clack, clickety clack. The transcontinental chariot sped onwards through forests of jack-pine and spruce, hemlock and fir. So many trees, so much space, this was a truly overwhelming vista.

The view from my window was a trio of vivid hues, a deep blue sky, a mantle of evergreen green, both colours in stark contrast to the virgin white carpet below. Though we flashed by at great speed, my memory is of an overwhelming sameness. But I was captivated by the sheer magnitude of this beautiful yet lonely wilderness.

Eventually, our train slowed down. We were entering Montreal where we were to stay overnight. Fifty four young British boys and girls scrambling off a train and being herded onto two coaches must have been of some concern to the public at large. While boarding the coach that was to take us to our hostel, some French speaking children jeered and shouted at us. I remember Ped coming to an abrupt halt by my side, his face registering confusion and then anger. Miss Clark, seeing a potential racial conflict, unceremoniously and hurriedly shoved Ped and myself onto the coach.

★ ★ ★

The next day, Alec and I found ourselves alone on the streets of Montreal. Inadvertently, we had slipped round some street corner and lost touch with the main party. But we were not over-concerned, what with an hour or so to spare and only five minutes at most from the railway station.

'Alec, let's ask that man over there which direction we take for the station. I think it's down this way, but we better make sure.'

Within seconds of crossing the road, we were suddenly swooped upon by a gang of kids. It was the first time either of us had seen so many black faces. It was alarming.

'Lets get 'em boys, and do 'em over,' one of the little guys in the middle of the bunch shouted as we were pressed hard up against a brick wall.

The man to whom I had intended to speak

was nowhere to be seen — help from this corner vanished with his lightning disappearance.

But soon aid came, sort of. The boy I'd seen barging his way through to the front suddenly spoke to us. 'If you kids got any money for us, we'll let you go.'

'I am sorry,' I replied, 'but we have not a penny between us. We've just come over from England and we are on our way to New York.'

'Holy mackerel, they're Limeys, just listen to their posh talk.'

'No, we are British,' I interrupted, 'and we need to get back to the railway station.'

'Jeezus, they are our allies, we don't hurt them,' said their leader, immediately exerting control over his unruly followers. Turning back to me, he continued: 'Say kid, yuh don't have one of those blazer buttons to spare as a souvenir, do yuh?'

Envisaging a happy ending to this unwanted confrontation, I was only too pleased to oblige, and thinking that my accent may keep this lot in a good humour, I replied in the most English manner I could muster: 'Of course, Old Bean. Show us the way to the station and you can have one from each of us.'

I assumed Alec would agree to my suggestion, but to my dismay, the same little so-and-so who had wanted to 'do us in', now squirmed eel-like to the front: 'I want a button too.'

Then a whole chorus of boyish voices joined in, all demanding a button. We ended up with buttonless blazers. Still, the gang were true to their word and led us back to the station where we parted on good terms.

Moreover, this unusual incident generated sympathy from our superiors and saved us from a telling-off, or worse. Alec and I were also very relieved to be back on the train in one piece.

While heading south to the American border, my memory of Montreal remains one of dreary coldness and fear, a mental picture I've been told was far from accurate.

★   ★   ★

At long last, our train chugged into Grand Central Station in New York City. Everywhere was hustle and bustle, with noisy people hurrying this way and that way with no time to spare.

We were herded onto two luxurious coaches. This was my first taste of the exaggerated razzmatazz of the American way of life.

Four speed cops, two up front and two in

the rear, guided us with sirens blazing, lights flashing through the streets of Manhattan and the Bronx, to our final destination: The Edwin Gould Foundation, 1760 Stillwell Avenue, The Bronx, New York, New York.

The institution consisted of five 'cottages', three of which were allocated to all fifty-four of us who had journeyed from England. We had our own swimming pool, playing fields, and even a hospital. In fact the whole of Stillwell Avenue seemed to belong to the Edwin Gould Foundation.

★   ★   ★

As it was, California was supposed to be our ultimate destination. As the offspring of British entertainers, the plan was that we would all be 'adopted' by Hollywood stars and live in Tinseltown.

But as soon as we arrived, a rotten rumour was buzzing about that this might be our permanent residence for the duration of the war.

Not many more days passed before this rumour was confirmed. Apparently, it was not to be. We weren't going to be living with the likes of Walter Pidgeon, Mary Pickford or Douglas Fairbanks after all. The initial plan was that various Hollywood families in

139

California were going to look after us for the duration of the war. Perhaps this was too ambitious an undertaking for the authorities. In any event, the final outcome was for us all to remain at the Edwin Gould Foundation with the acting fraternity supplying financial support.

To me it seemed cruel to tell us we were going to be integrated into family life in California, and then within a few weeks to have all our hopes dashed and have to face yet more institutional existence for the next few years to come.

I was terribly disappointed. And for the next few days, I lamented my tragic fate. But being young and resilient like the others, I quickly resigned myself and made the best of it. Not that I had a lot of choice.

★　★　★

Those of us not old enough to go to Christopher Columbus High School straight away, had to attend 'Public School Eighty-eight' at Pelham Bay, otherwise known as P.S.88. The school was located within walking distance of the 'Edwin Gould' which was on the outer edge of the Bronx. It was a tough school situated in a working class area. An area dominated by the subway, which carried the trains that rattled along high above the houses on huge concrete pillars. Before the first week was over, I knew I was going to have to fight the school bully. Not only did our personalities clash, but because I was small for my age, he assumed I was easy meat. My short trousers only served to exacerbate the situation. This wasn't the first time that wearing shorts misled some of the local kids into assuming we were pushovers. The American kids in the school wore either long trousers or knickerbockers. But our orphanage life from a tender age had conditioned us to be tough and hard when necessary. What this big bully had not realised was that I was very strong for my size, and quick with it.

I hated fighting, and was not looking forward to the inevitable encounter, but I had long since learned that survival in the world I knew, was to meet a bully headon.

Predictably, matters came to a head one day at break time in the playground, or should I say battleground.

The bumptious lout came swaggering over, flanked by two of his cronies.

'Hey, Limey,' he taunted. 'Only sissies wear short trousers.'

I was definitely on a short fuse. He had no time to say another word. I flew straight at him with such force we both fell to the ground. Although he was a lot bigger and heavier than me, this sort of fighting was alien to him. Nor was he as strong as he appeared. In fact, he was much softer than I.

In no time at all I had him locked in my favourite hold, a neck grip — a position where his extra weight was rendered useless. The fight lasted no more than a minute from the time he opened his mouth until he gave in.

★   ★   ★

After that, my remaining few months at P.S.88 were very enjoyable and I made a lot of friends as a result of taking on and beating the school bully.

At about the same time, by sheer coincidence, Leonard, one of the bigger orphan boys from 'B' cottage was having a similar problem.

★   ★   ★

Three boys were taking the mickey out of him in the high school. But Len was very solid, hard and had an unusually high density of muscle (this was probably why he could not swim. No matter how many times he tried, he just sank). No one in our orphanage crossed Len, nor needed to, for he was a nice guy.

These three boys must have thought an express train had hit them. By the time they dragged Len away, two of them were taken to the school infirmary for treatment.

Nevertheless, these two fights had two positive results for all the boys in the Foundation. First, we gained some 'respect' in the eyes of the local boys, and second, we no longer had to wear short pants and were allowed to dress like our American counterparts.

This decision suited us well. Not only were American clothes more comfortable, but now we blended in.

* * *

While I was at P.S.88 I made a good friend with an American boy of Italian descent named Ralph Fratiani. He tutored me in the art of riding the New York subway system, a useful addition to my education.

Ralph was tall for his age, slim, dark and softly spoken, but very streetwise. And he had an uncanny knack of keeping out of trouble, a necessary skill for when only the two of us were riding the subway.

Whenever the opportunity arose, we

travelled in the front carriage and had a perfect view as the train wound its way under the city.

★ ★ ★

Ralph had a way of making a nickel take us from one end of New York to the other and back again. So I soon knew my way underground far better than on the streets above.

There was one time when Ralph and I were in the front of the subway and all the other passengers had alighted. Suddenly, a rowdy crowd of young kids headed for the doors of our carriage. Ralph immediately jumped up and told me to follow quickly. The urgency in his voice had me close behind him in a jiffy. We jumped out the door, just as the unruly gang poured into the other one.

Ralph had recognised one of the kids, and their gang was quite a nasty bunch, especially when the odds were three-to-one in their favour. When we were safely ensconced in a more crowded part of the train, Ralph said: 'Bergie, when you ride the subway alone, look out for who is in the carriage and who's gonna get on.'

This was all part of my education, of course, however practical.

★ ★ ★

Within a month or two of having settled down at Christopher Columbus, I and a few others had a day off from school. We were camping out in the White Plains area for a long weekend. I particularly remember our railway journey — not the usual kind where you sit on a seat in relative comfort, with an engine pulling you and your carriage to a pre-determined destination. No, this was a more energetic, cheaper mode of travel.

In any case, Giff and I were strolling contentedly along a little-used railway track but continually wondering what was round the next bend. But all that seemed to be round the next bend was another bend. The curves kept coming and going, all pretty similar . . . except one.

While this curve displayed no change of scenery, we were suddenly facing a gang of boys heading in our direction. A confrontation between the two parties was unavoidable.

Giff and I held the inside of the track, and two of their lads were doing likewise. Both groups halted and stood waiting for one or other to give way. For a few interminable seconds, four boys steadfastly holding their

145

share of the railway sleepers, stood stock still. Thoughts of Robin Hood confronting Little John flashed through my mind.

It was their move.

Then the biggest of the boys said belligerently: 'Where you guys from?'

'We're on holiday,' I retorted with equal belligerence. 'Where are you from?' I was damned if I was gonna be bullied by strange kids no older than myself.

'Round and about,' the big boy answered, glaring aggressively, confident in the fact he was tall enough to dictate terms. His size didn't worry me, it was more his gang's numerical superiority causing me concern.

'Well, we don't want any trouble, so if you two kids' (pointing to Giff and I) 'move over we'll be on our way.'

Until now, Giff had been silent, but no longer. Giff was two years older than me, and the toughest guy in our group.

'You got one helluva long wait, fella, if you think I'm gonna move on your say-so', Giff said evenly.

The big guy was somewhat taken aback. But having crossed the Rubicon, he moved menacingly towards Giff.

'Now, listen Bud, I don't wanna hurt you, so just step aside. There's no sense in you getting all riled up. Beat it, before I get really annoyed.'

★ ★ ★

My money was on Giff. I was willing to bet he was tougher than their leader. Giff thought so too and widened his stance on the track. I moved over closer to Giff to display an air of solidarity.

'Move out the way Bergie, this is between me and this loud-mouthed bloke.'

Our champ against theirs. But the big guy was no pushover.

Even so, Giff would surely have come out the winner if fate hadn't intervened so cruelly. Rolling over and over on the dusty ground, I noticed Giff's face was suddenly contorted in pain.

The big guy was happy to let go. He had had enough.' Your chap's hurt so let's shake hands and we'll be on our way,' he said, glad to save face. With Giff in a bad state, we were happy to oblige. So both parties parted amicably with honour in tact all round.

Giff gingerly rose to his feet.

'What was the matter, Giff? You had him easy,' I cried. 'What went wrong?'

'I dunno, something hurt real bad

right up my backside.'

He could hardly walk, and no wonder. While wrestling on the ground, a sliver of stone had pierced his bottom between his cheeks, and for the next few days, Giff was out of commission, having a slightly embarrassing time in the hospital.

9

The Haunted House

'Come on, you three, you're late again,' said the good-natured Ray. Ray Zieg was a young American man, employed by the Edwin Gould Foundation as a sort of chauffeur-cum-handyman. He sometimes drove us about in the little old yellow school bus. That morning, we hurriedly clambered aboard, wended our way to the rear and squeezed into the back seat.

Another Sunday, and as usual we were chugging along towards Pelham Manor to go to church.

Pelham Manor smiled on me whereas Pelham Bay in the Bronx frowned most of the time. Consequently I was never able to relax there.

For example, one day, young Jason and I were outside roller-skating somewhere near a main road which led into town. Suddenly, two boys approached us.

'Hey kids, which is the best way to Fordham?'

Jason happily obliged whereupon one of

the boys hit him in the mouth.

'That's how we say thank you in Fordham,' he said before they both ran off across the grass.

I always looked forward to going to church, mainly because of their breakfasts. On each plate at breakfast time there was a big bunch of seedless grapes and added to this luxury, a choice of crackling cold cereals with dough-nuts and coffee.

I also had another reason for liking this particular church, although I never told a living soul. The girls were so pretty in their expensive clothes. One girl in particular, I had a crush on. Her name was Winnie Sexton, but I never even had the courage to speak to her.

I was just beginning to realise that girls were more interesting than I had been led to believe.

There was one of our own girls I liked very much, but unfortunately I was too immature to compete with an American boy who was three years older than I. Her name was Ursula and, even now, I often wonder where she is.

Yes, Pelham Manor was a great place. Not only was it the home of my scout troop, but the people were so friendly to us. Indeed, so different was its way of life to Pelham Bay in the Bronx, I often prayed to God that I may live there with a family.

★　★　★

It was Chris who first suggested that we go and investigate the notorious haunted house that people keep talking about.

'Yeah, let's,' Ped chimed in with his usual enthusiasm.

'Listen,' Chris continued, 'when we get off the bus we can nip round the side of the church and hide behind the big gravestones until everybody has gone inside. But, for God's sake, don't be seen.'

'For whose sake?' I asked, glancing at Ped, who was struggling not to laugh.

'Have I said anything funny? What the hell are you two guys laughing at?' There were times when Chris was so intense that humour passed him by.

'It's a good idea, Chris,' I said, though I was reluctant to go along because I didn't really want to miss my breakfast. But I went along nevertheless.

The house was big and very old. We slipped through the rusting iron gates and slowly made our way across what was once a huge garden full of all sorts of overgrown exotic shrubs and herbaceous flower borders, that

151

were now all but wild.

The air seemed much cooler and for the first time since entering the garden, I noticed the silence. Not even a bird twittered.

After hacking our way through the tangled and matted undergrowth, we stopped to rest in the only available clearing — a grassy knoll topped by an old cherry tree.

Was it my imagination, or was the silence becoming even more oppressive? An eerie stillness seeped into our immediate surroundings, and looking again at the gnarled and ugly old cherry tree, I suppressed a cold shiver.

'Look, Chris,' my voice croaked and broke the quiet so suddenly that poor old Ped tripped forward over a half exposed tree root. 'I've never seen such tiny cherries.'

'That's because the tree has reverted back to it's wild state,' said Chris with an air of superiority.

'I know that. I went to that nature lesson too!' I retorted sarcastically. 'But look how red all the cherries are, there's not an unripe one to be seen. This sure is a spooky tree. And see also how the branches point in one direction.'

'That's because of the prevailing wind, you dope,' Chris replied.

'I don't know about you two guys,' said

Ped. 'All I know is that darn tree sure points in one direction and that's straight towards the house. Prevailing wind or not, I find that a bit weird. I vote we go down to the bay for a spell.'

Chris and I didn't need any further persuading, so all three of us started walking to the end of the garden which swept majestically in a gentle curve down to the water's edge. The rickety old dock was in an even worse state than the rest of the garden. It was obvious from its rotting boards jutting above the water line that the pier had been out of commission for a long time.

'Jeepers, getting to the other end of the pier is gonna take some doing,' I exclaimed.

'Go on, Bergie, you're lightest, you go first,' chirped Chris.

'Off you go,' Ped chimed in. 'We'll fish you out if this lot collapses.'

Trying to ignore my fears, I gingerly led the way to the other end of the pier. 'For crying out loud Chris, don't wobble it so much,' I cried.

When we'd gotten halfway across, Ped's cry stopped us dead.

'Where did he come from?' I asked terrified that he might join us on the pier and sink us with his weight.

'Never mind that, Bergie, look at his

clothes. They're a bit queer don't you think?'

His coat appeared miles too big, for it came almost down to his knees and had large cuffs on the end of his sleeves. His hat was peculiar as well, like a cloth boat perched on top of his head. His trousers ended just below his knees where his long socks took over, running the rest of the way down his leg, all the way to his pointed shoes.

As we stood on the now quivering jetty (I think it was we three doing the quivering) the old man came slowly onwards and without hesitating in his stride, stepped effortlessly onto the pier and proceeded with a mincing stride in our direction.

Not a ripple of water lapped over the edge of the boards as he strode purposefully ever nearer. It was the most menacing and sinister sight I had ever encountered and I knew I wasn't dreaming. Never had I felt so trapped, not even that time I slipped and fell into the bog and these same two companions fished me out from the filthy swamp which had me trapped up to my armpits.

Strike a light! I thought in terror. Just supposing he is a ghost? For the first time, I thought this whole wretched place might be haunted after all. Oh God, I thought, why didn't I go to church?

The odd old man, who beggared description, stopped and deliberately took up a straddled stance to counter the swaying of the pier.

'We were just exploring,' I said as forcefully as I could manage.

'Huh! is that so? Do you know what happened to the last boy who went exploring in this forbidden area?' the figment said.

'No, of course you don't, ha ha ha, otherwise you wouldn't be here now,' he started laughing in a funny cackling sort of way.

'Well, you silly little middens, I'll tell you. A boy no older than you three kids was pulled out of this very bay, a while back. He'd bin chopped to pieces, but what was real puzzlin' to the police was that he'd been put back together again with barbed wire.'

'With barbed wire?' we croaked in unison.

'Yep, with barbed wire, ha ha ha, all neatly skewered back into place he was, a dextrous job to be sure.'

The strange and frightening man scratched his chin and caressed his pointed beard.

'The strange thing was,' the old man continued, 'I never could figure out why whoever put him together so clever like, got the hands mixed up.' He started laughing again with that weird cackle. 'I guess he had

155

one helluva sense of humour. Now you guys had better just scram, else you never know what might happen to you. And by the way,' he shouted, for we were already halfway towards the shore, 'Whatever you do, don't eat the cherries from the forbidden tree!'

Still guffawing and cackling, the strange old man with the strange old clothes and the strange old accent turned and carried on to the end of the slipway.

We ran back to the grassy knoll, stopped and turned round.

'You know what,' Chris said in a slightly breathless but belligerent tone,' I reckon that old grisly man is as mad as can be.'

'Maybe yes, maybe no, but there's one thing for certain, he ain't there no more,' Ped replied in awe. The old man had vanished.

'Now where the hell did he disappear to? Sod it,' I swore.' All that malarkey about barbed wire and cherry trees may or may not be true, but I'm kinda hungry and I'm gonna eat some of them cherries.'

'Yeah, me too.' Ped had already grabbed a handful but Chris declined, explaining that cherries gave him a tummy ache, plus he liked strawberries better anyway.

Half choking on a cherry, Ped suddenly cried out: 'Look, Bergie, look! there's a face up there, quick!'

I spun round nearly jumping out of my skin, and just for long enough to be certain, but no longer, I too caught a glimpse of the face before the heavy curtain fell back into place.

'Stop mucking about, you two, it's making me jumpy,' Chris bleated.

'Honest Chris, it's the truth,' I said, describing what I had seen at the top right hand window.

Despite the fact that a fleeting glimpse was all I had, our separate descriptions tallied down to the last detail.

The face belonged to a very old woman. A wrinkled face, longish, with a thin prominent nose, which seemed to hover over a wide narrow mouth. To this day, I still swear the face was real. Ped, who had a moment or two longer look than I, swore that she was wearing some sort of black cloak.

Ped and I reckoned that two ghosts were enough excitement for one day, and we were happy to go back to church. Besides if we hurried, we might still make it for breakfast. But Chris had other ideas.

'Come on, you guys. You've got to prove to me that you're right' he said bravely. 'But I don't want to go in there alone.'

I looked at Ped.

'Okay, let's go and find out. Cor, it must be

the cherries you blokes ate. I never saw any blinking face,' Chris said sceptically.

* * *

Ped picked up a good sized stick that he hopefully thought would be a match for any ghost, and without more ado, we walked up to the rambling, dilapidated old house.

The bottom windows were all boarded up and yet the front door was ajar. Why? I wondered. We carefully squeezed our way inside, the stale dank air intermingling with an eerie coldness that seemed to envelop our bodies in an invisible blanket.

Again I felt very jittery and judging from their faces, Chris and Ped were just as scared.

But in spite of the dim light, we had no trouble finding the stairs, for they were straight ahead of us.

'Here we go,' I whispered. There was no turning back now. I knew that we would have to visit that room on the top floor. The other two agreed, so each of us armed with what we hoped were suitable weapons to defend ourselves, crept carefully up the winding staircase.

So far, so good. We were on the top landing. I took a deep breath, walked over to the door and slowly turned the King-sized glass handle and very carefully pushed it open.

The room was empty.

But wait, what was that under the window? Under the same window where Ped first glimpsed the old lady's face, a little pile of clothes, old woman's clothes from a past era, were lying on the floor as though somebody had hurriedly disrobed.

Ped went across the room and poked the clothes about with his stick. I was just trying to work out why he was doing this when we suddenly froze to the spot.

We had all heard the noise simultaneously. A screaming banshee, wailing in the middle of the night could not have made us any more fearful. With our hearts thumping madly, we ran out of the room and stood absolutely still, unable to move.

Again we heard heavy footsteps purposefully pacing to and fro below. We knew that whoever or whatever was down there was sooner or later going to come up the staircase. I felt numb.

We waited for what was like an eternity and then, what we all knew was going to happen, happened. My hair was on end.

I could here the measured tread of a heavy man, slowly and methodically climbing the stairs. On and on came the deliberate footfalls, stepping upwards, nearer and nearer.

Ped who could not contain himself any longer leaned over the banister.

'Strewth, its a bloody cop!' he cried, 'and he's got a gun.'

There was no time to think.

'Hello officer,' I said, 'We thought we saw a face at the window and we came to have a look, sorry if we've caused you any trouble.'

'Well, I'll be damned,' exclaimed the policeman, taking his peaked cap from his head. 'What in tarnation are you three kids doing here. This is not a healthy place to be. They say the whole area is haunted. I don't believe in ghosts myself, but I gotta admit there have been a few unexplained happenings here over the years. Yessiree, a very unsavoury part of Pelham Manor is this. The sooner they demolish this house, the better.'

'Please Sir,' I interrupted. 'That was the room where we saw the face, but when we came in to investigate, all we saw was some old clothes where the lady had been standing under the window, and . . . '

'Okay,' he said, walking into the room. 'So where are these clothes then?'

We were dumbfounded. I just stared and stared at the spot where only minutes earlier there had been a neat little pile of ancient clothes. Ped and I were in a complete state of shock. Ped kept looking at his stick, and then back again at the floor and Chris looked bewildered.

'I swear they were just there a minute ago, weren't they Bergie?' Ped had found his voice again.

I nodded. 'It's the truth Sir, I even poked them with my stick,' Ped said.

'Well, if this don't beat all. Where you kids from? Sure as hell not round here.'

I looked at Ped.

'We're from the Edwin Gould Foundation in the Bronx, sir,' I explained, 'but on Sundays we come . . . '

The burly cop finished the sentence for me. 'Here to church. I might have known you were those British evacuees. Now listen to me. This is not the place for young lads, or anyone else for that matter. I've heard tell that this house had a curse put on it years ago. So get the hell out of here, and don't come back, or you might end up being fished out of the bay like the unlucky boy a while back,' he said, glancing at his watch. 'Hurry up so as not to miss your bus.'

'Thanks sir, goodbye Officer,' we all shouted in chorus as we tore down the stairs and headed back to the churchyard as fast as our legs could carry us.

As impressionable young boys, we naturally believed the house was really haunted, and we never went near it again.

Years later, I learned that the house had long ago been a house of ill-repute, visited by some of the richest people in the area, a place where tragedy and mayhem had often occurred.

Even so, I often searched for a logical explanation for what we saw for surely there must have been one. But I have never been able to produce a satisfactory theory to explain the events that occurred on that fine late summer's day.

10

The Runaways

'Come on Bergie! It's time,' whispered Chris, trying to keep his voice down. Unfortunately, his efforts resulted in a rasping shout, almost as loud as his natural voice.

'Can't you hear the clock? It's striking midnight!' he said, now almost shouting with excitement.

'Okay, okay, I'm awake.' I responded.

Three whole hours of intensive planning were now coming to fruition and our journey, which we naively hoped would end in Texas, was about to begin.

We'd often heard stories about British prisoners of war escaping or attempting to escape from the Germans. Now it was our turn to become fugitives from grown-up tyranny.

Skilfully, I tied a clove-hitch to the bedstead with my sheet and, with a reef-knot, joined Ped's to mine. If nothing else, this sure was going to be a dramatic escape.

'Toss the home-made rope out of the window, and you go first Ped.'

'Why me, Bergie?'

'Well, hmmm . . . you're heavier than I am and if the sheets take your weight we're all safe,' I reasoned. 'If I went first, we still wouldn't know if they would hold your weight.'

Chris nodded in agreement.

'Are you saying I'm fat?' Ped exclaimed.

'Good God, no, its just that you're bigger than I am.'

'For God's sake, hurry up,' Chris insisted.

Soon Ped's head disappeared over the window sill followed by the rest of us.

★　★　★

For the first few miles we knew our way and despite the darkness, our route was easy to follow.

The days of P.S.88 were behind us.

So was Christopher Columbus High School which had been our place of learning for more than two years now. The school was a huge Comprehensive and due to its size, there was great difficulty in keeping track of all the teachers, let alone the pupils.

Although C.C.H.S. was a fair distance from the Foundation, we walked to and fro every day. But now it was good riddance . . .

How well I remember that first winter walking to school. It was cold. Ear muffs, parkas and mittens were our regular attire.

One freezing day, no sooner had I entered the school entrance than I began to feel dizzy. By the time I entered the corridor, I knew I was in trouble. I never reached the classroom. When I woke up, I found myself in the infirmary.

'What happened to me, nurse?'

The nurse explained to me that coming from a temperature of ten degrees below zero Fahrenheit (minus 23°C) into a centrally heated building of 70 degrees Fahrenheit (21°C) had caused me to faint. Nor was I the first one to succumb to this sudden temperature change this winter.

But I acclimatised quite quickly because apart from three almost frost-bitten fingers due to carrying my textbooks in one position for too long, the coldest of days never bothered me after that.

There was no comparison between the discipline at Christopher Columbus High School and the Actors' Orphanage in England. Although this was a welcome change in a lot of respects, it was certainly a pity from an educational viewpoint. But then, how could a comprehensive school with 4000 pupils compete with an English-style Public school, with just 80 boys and girls?

★ ★ ★

It was at the end of the summer term, when six of us were summoned to the Superintendent's office, and that could mean only one thing . . . trouble.

'In all my life I have never ever read such a dreadful set of school reports,' the 'Super' said. 'Do you boys realise they are so bad that I find them difficult to believe? You are a disgrace to your country. Do you boys, in your wildest dreams, expect to get away with such marks? Somebody, please say there is a mistake somewhere.'

'Oh there probably w . . . '

'SHUTUP HUGO!'

A deathly silence followed.

'Let me read your term marks, bearing in mind that 65% is the absolute minimum required to pass. Hugo: English 40%, Geometry 30%, French 25% . . . '

'Excuse me, Sir.'

'One more word from you Hugo and you'll be in even hotter water!'

By now one or two muffled sniggers from further down the line were audible. (I only wanted to say that the French mark was terribly unfair because our teacher, being French herself, was not very enamoured with the British, especially with Ped and I, it seemed. At first I thought this was because Ped and I were personally to blame for General Wolf storming the heights of Quebec, but I was wrong. I found out later that the evacuation of Dunkirk is what really bugged her. At the moment anything English was not very popular with my French teacher. Come to think of it, Mr Griffin wasn't exactly pleased with us either).

Christopher's marks were much the same as mine, but Claude's were so bad that it was becoming increasingly difficult not to burst out laughing.

Then came Peter de Redder's report.

'English 35% (his highest mark), Geometry 23%, French 15%.'

Poor old Ped, we could not stifle our giggles any longer.

'Stop it, stop laughing this instant,' thundered Mr. Griffin, but it was too late. We were now laughing uncontrollably.

Then, about ten seconds later, amidst complete pandemonium: Thwack, Thud! I didn't know what hit me.

The thwack was old Griff's hand connecting with a certain part of my anatomy, and the following thud was the far wall of his office meeting with another part. Old Griff certainly did pack a wallop.

Soon we were filing out of his office, my head still ringing and still not knowing whether there was any more punishment to be dished out in the future.

In my heart of hearts I realised that this episode was only an excuse to abscond. As far as I was concerned there were more serious reasons.

★   ★   ★

An unearthly silence descended over the three of us, an enveloping emptiness and quietness blanketed the surrounding country-side. Dawn was still a fair way off. Trudging on, my mind wandered once more. I thought of the many different reasons why I was running away, not that I regarded this escape as running away, but rather as a great adventure, a challenge which I gladly accepted.

★   ★   ★

Now amidst the predawn chill, my mind wandered back to another episode.

Once one of the older boys persuaded some of the smaller and younger lads to gang up and jump on a boy he didn't like, then hold him down so he could beat all hell out of him. In an ironic twist, Donald, the unfortunate victim, was taken out of the Edwin Gould Foundation and placed with a very nice family.

As for Bob, the one responsible for the incident, he lost the respect even of the kids who initially thought it would only be a good ragging. I still find it difficult to feel any warmth for him, even though the event was a lifetime away.

I always hated fighting. Bullies I could cope with, canings were a piece of cake (although they expired when we left England) but violence among lads you lived with twenty four hours a day, I could not tolerate. Oversensitive, yes. Naive, maybe. But this was just one of many reasons for my departure without permission.

'Hey, Bergie, let's climb up onto the Parkway and hitch a lift. If we're lucky we'll be miles away before it gets light.'

We scrambled up the embankment and started to thumb our way further west.

Perhaps a quarter of an hour had gone by and not a sign of a car. The road was empty, not even a street light pierced the darkness. All three of us pressed on, all the while locked in our own private reflections.

I again thought back to the High School. My PE teacher, Mr. Schoenfield had given me 90%. Jumping jellyfish!

'Hey you guys, old Griff only mentioned our rotten grades, not the good ones.' No answer was forthcoming from my two companions, still wrapped up in their own thoughts.

Then another memory. I was walking to school when this mad squirrel attacked me, or perhaps it just fell out of a tree on top of me. In any case, the vicious little critter landed on my head and when I put my hand up, it bit my finger to the bone. It hurt like hell.

We all stood there watching it wriggling this way and that, still dangling with a grip like a powerful bulldog. The blasted tree-rat just wouldn't let go until Ralph gave it a couple of hefty thumps which finally persuaded it to run off somewhere.

★ ★ ★

An hour later, a car slowed down almost to a halt. But as we ran towards it, the driver zoomed off.

'What a rotten sod,' exclaimed Chris, 'why

did he buzz off like that?' Ped answered with a grunt and just kept on walking. That's what endeared me to Ped, his steadfastness and unflappability in most situations.

Actually I was a little worried about the car.

'Don't worry, Bergie, we can always hide in the ditch if another car comes by.' The fact that it was dark would probably be to our advantage, so I forgot all about it.

By now, conversation was minimal.

Soon a faint greyish light was slowly fingering its way across the eastern sky, shedding an eerie light over the dark, dank swamps to our left. I shivered and with good reason. Swamps held a very unpleasant memory for me. After all, it was only a year earlier that these same two companions with me now had hauled me out of a smelly old bog. The suction was mighty powerful. I had fallen in and was up to my waist in a jiffy and sinking fast when they grabbed hold of me.

'Hold on, you guys, I'm gonna take a compass bearing,' I said.

It was then that we heard the police siren, faintly at first, but the wailing increased in intensity every second.

'Holy mackerel! Quick boys, its the cops,' I yelled. 'How did they get on to us so quickly?'

Our legs fairly flew over the ground as the

three of us ran down the bank into the fields, still heading westward to the 'Lone Star State'. Fortune was with us in the shape of a bush. We crouched low and peered through the foliage at the police car as it sped by.

'It looks like they didn't see us,' Chris's whispered with relief. 'They sure made a mistake switching on their siren, else they could have come up on us and we would have been dead ducks.'

'Yep,' Ped agreed, 'what say you take a compass bearing west-south-west and we can do a beeline hike for a while.'

'Yeah, a good idea' I agreed as I fished out my spare lumberjack shirt for protection against the damp foggy atmosphere that had risen from the boggy ground in the early morning hours.

And so we headed into unknown territory.

Behind us the Eastern sky was clearly visible and dawn's early light was fast creeping ever closer to where we three were still in shadow.

We could just make out a country lane roughly twenty yards distant.

'Hang on, guys, we got a problem,' said Chris. 'If the cops were tipped off by the stinker in the car last night, we're in trouble and we'll have to stay out of sight somewhere.'

'I guess so.' we agreed, without enthusiasm.

'On the other hand,' Chris continued, 'if it was just routine police work, or the siren wasn't meant for us, we're in the clear for at least another hour or so, and by that time, we should reach the railway line and can jump the next freight.'

Personally I was in favour of going hell for leather for the railway line. But any decision we were about to make was irrelevant, for suddenly we were almost blinded by a police search light.

'Stay where you are,' came the voice over the loudspeaker. We kept running.

'Do you kids want a forty-five up your ass?'

We had reached the end of the road. All our romantic ideas of becoming cowboys in Texas had been flattened. We walked dejectedly back to the waiting police cars.

'Crikey, those guns are big enough to blow our heads off. I wonder if they really would have shot at us,' I whispered.

Two or three powerful flashlights in the hands of the police flitted over us from head to toe.

'Well, I'll be damned, if that don't beat all. Surely to God, my eyes must be deceiving me.' A burly cop with a faintly familiar voice stepped forward, lifted his cap and palmed through his hair before replacing it.

'By God, it is them. It's the same three Limeys I ran into in Pelham Manor a while back. You three sure have a talent for turning up in the queerest of places.'

He turned to his colleagues and showered them with the details of our meeting in the haunted house, which was received with guffaws of laughter.

'You'll have to come with me this time boys. I'm taking you back to the Institute. No doubt, your boss will deal with you. There's no need for this to be a police matter.'

One of the other cops cut in: 'Where were you boys heading for anyway?'

'Texas,' we said in unison.

More laughter. Mac, the policeman, took command again.

'Well, boys, two hundred years ago if you had been heading West, you'd have had all our blessings, but right now just hop into the car cos you're all going back to your present home.'

The Law escorted us all the way back to the Foundation and treated us really well. Even old Griff was relieved, having been notified in advance that we were on our way home, safe and sound.

He was waiting for us on arrival.

'Oh, Boys,' he said, 'what am I going to do with you three? And what's with the

174

bed-sheets and night escape, why in hell's name didn't you wait for the weekend? Who knows, you may even have reached the state line before we missed you. At least your imaginations must be better than average! Now listen to me good. You've had your fun and your share of trouble, but this little escapade of yours must never happen again, do you boys understand me?'

'Yes, sir,' we cried in unison.

'Running away is a very serious and dangerous matter, so thank your lucky stars the three of you are back in one piece. Believe me, there are enough dangers lurking out there in the daytime, let alone at night. Oh! and by the way, do better at school next term or I will have your guts for garters. Now get going.'

'Hey, fellas, that's a good idea.' I said.

'What is?'

'Next time we will wait for a weekend.'

11

The Black Widow

My days at the Boy Scout Camp Siwanoy were among the happiest of my childhood.

Siwanoy was formerly a Red Indian reservation deep in the foothills of the Catskill Mountains in New York state, a region as large as the whole of England. And I'd been fortunate enough to spend my summers there.

Back in the 1940s, however, the place could be wild, lonesome, beautiful. And dangerous.

Nobody had warned me about spiders. Nor had anyone warned me about the deadliest of them all.

It was late June, and I'd been looking forward to another carefree summer in the idyllic mountains. Yet even now I remember the awful pain . . . pain so intense I kept pleading with the doctor to finish his daily drainage operations quickly so he wouldn't see me cry.

'You know, Doc,' I said, 'I hate you when you come in every morning, but I sure love you when you're gone.'

'You ungrateful little limey,' he chuckled in his funny accent.

He was good, that medicine man. He saved my life.

Still, I wondered what brought this Austrian doctor to these lonely hills. He revealed nothing of his recent past, but from the snatches of conversation I overheard, I gathered that Adolf Hitler was involved. I supposed that being Jewish meant he had to leave the country in a hurry. Although he was happy to talk about his childhood, he kept those few years before the war to himself.

For the first time in my life, I realised how lucky I was to be alive. So in tune with the magic of Siwanoy was my mind and body that being bedridden made no difference to the happiness I felt. As I lay on my pillow, the fragrant scent of jack-pine and wild flowers wafted gently through the cabin hospital window and my mind drifted back to a recent afternoon when I was roaming the foothills on a mountain pony.

The warm sun was high in the heavens and my scout troop was heading for the higher peaks in the distance and I was thrilled to be touching the sweaty thick neck of my sure-footed pony as he warily picked his way along the mountainous trail. Suddenly, as we curved sharply to the right, we found ourselves in a large clearing. It seemed the ideal spot to rein in our horses and take a breather. Mac, our leader, thought so too.

'This is a good place to make camp for the day,' he told the six of us. 'We'll stay the night and go back the long way round tomorrow. After you have all attended to your horses and paired off, the rest of the day is yours. Whitey, you pair off with Bergie. I know that's what you're hankering to do anyway.'

This was the chance I had been praying for.

'Please, Mac, may I buzz off and practise my pathfinding for a spell? I have to take my test next week and it will be fine practise for me up here.'

The Pathfinder badge meant a lot to me. Apart from being one of the most coveted badges, it was also necessary to move up the ladder to the ultimate goal — becoming an Eagle Scout. But that was a long way off. For now, I was thinking about the final exam, where you were dropped off some miles from camp and had to find your way back within a certain time.

Mac considered my request: 'I don't think its a good idea Bergie, cos you've never been alone in the Catskills before.'

'Please Mac, I know he's a limey,' Whitey

interrupted, 'but he's good with a compass, and I've taught him to read the mountains real well. Besides, he might not get another chance this year, leastways, not this high up.'

'Honest to God, Mac, I'll take lots of bearings, and mark the trails real good,' I pleaded. 'And besides, I'll be the first English guy in the troop to get this badge.'

'Hmmm . . . Okay,' Mac relented. 'But you gotta be back in three hours.'

'Thanks a million, Mac. Hey, Whitey, do me a favour, look after my horse and have some coffee on the go when I get back.'

'Don't meet up with a bear,' joked Whitey. Or was he joking? I thought that in high summer, bears were much further north.

But we waved goodbye nevertheless, and I hit the trail in a westerly direction. Nearly every time I went roaming, I headed West. For me, it was the most romantic point of the compass.

★   ★   ★

As I strolled slowly away from my companions, I was captivated by the beauty. All I could see, touch, hear, and smell, merged harmoniously into one glorious sensation that has haunted me pleasantly ever since. Never did a musician hear such a beautiful symphony as I heard that day in the mountains. Silently I moved further and further into a blissful loneliness.

Then instinctively, I trailed a wasp's flight path which led me to the blackened ruins of an old log cabin and stepping gingerly over the charred remains, I sat down in what I assumed was the middle. There I watched woodlice grubbing through a rotting log at my feet and crickets furiously rubbing their legs together to make their distinctive sound while high above me in the clear, blue sky, the sweet sharp notes of skylarks and other winged creatures sounded above the treetops.

At that moment, the Bronx orphanage was a million miles away. I was in paradise.

Lazily, I rolled over on my tummy and with the sun warming my body, my thoughts strayed into fantasy and I drifted off.

Time spun backwards. Magically, the burnt cabin took on its original shape. A lone trapper slumped over a crude table with the haft and feathers of an arrow protruding from his back. Nearby, savage yells mixed with the crackling hiss of burning logs as a half-naked man fled the holocaust with a few pelts. Flames licked and leapt and finally engulfed all in its path. The heat was unbearable, and as I woke from sleep, I felt the sun, now at its height, beating down mercilessly on my back.

I got to my feet, strangely disturbed and excited by the dream. Looking round, I asked myself, was this the cabin of my dream? Were these few charred rotting timbers the remnants of an ancient trapper's home? Regardless, I wasn't going to tell Whitey. He'd say his limey friend has gone soft in the head from too much sun.

Without a backward glance, I strode into the late afternoon of the most beautiful day I could ever have hoped for.

★   ★   ★

The throbbing in my leg brought me back to the present, though the pain didn't seem quite as bad as it had been.

Lying in bed, I listened for the voices that would soon be coming up the trail, happy excited young voices. Voices belonging to boys I had been able to choose as friends which is a luxury not easy to find when you are living in an institution.

Yet every day, without fail, they came to see me, bringing ice-cold cokes — cokes so cold that only the Devil's Bathtub could have been responsible for their low temperature. Brrruh! the Devil's Bathtub was an icy hole, nestled far into the rocks and boulders and fed by minute mountain streams that bubbled up from the depths. A dark and mystical place, no scout worthy of his rank ever came to Siwanoy and dodged the excruciating thrill of bathing in nature's coldest, most invigorating pool.

I thought back to my first day and night at camp that year. I had just joined the infamous 'Larry Bug Queue', along with all the other silly boys who had succumbed to the symptoms of excessive consumption of fresh corn-cobs. But what could be more memorable and enjoyable than freshly boiled cobs of corn, smeared with salt and butter, eaten round an evening campfire? Or an imaginative yarn spun by a Scout leader as we sat in a circle, gazing into the blackness of the night?

★ ★ ★

It happened while I was waiting my turn to enter the latrines in a circular queue (circular because after one had finished his business, he would join in once more at the back of the line — such was the power of the larry bug).

It was on my third and final round in the queue that it happened. Just before entering the latrine again, I felt a sharp prick on the inside of my left leg, just above the knee. Glancing downwards, despite the dimness of the light, I saw a black spider. Unconcerned, I

182

hastily brushed it away with my hand. At that moment, a spider bite seemed of very little consequence especially as it was taking all my concentration to cope with a rumbling rectum.

A couple of hours later, however, I was dragging a very swollen and painful leg up the trail to the hospital cabin. The last thing I ever expected was to have to spend the rest of that year's Siwanoy holiday on my back.

The log cabin had three rooms, one for the doctor, one for his patients and one for a tiny dispensary, which was woefully inadequate for dealing with a person bitten by a Black Widow spider.

When I told the doctor what happened, he ordered me straight to bed. Soon I had a high fever and was feeling very strange indeed.

Not long after, my pals were racing to see me and find out if the rumours were true.

'Fancy being bitten by a black widow, Bergie,' said Whitey, sounding rather impressed. 'I hear tell they're more deadly than a rattlesnake, especially the female.'

'Huh?' I mumbled.

The doctor then came in from the dispensary and ordered Whitey to wait outside.

'It is true, you know, you have been bitten by a poisonous spider,' he said.

Now, along with feeling very ill, I was alarmed.

'Look, son, I'm going to have to operate on your leg very shortly,' the doctor said, his accent now heavier than ever. 'There's no time to have you taken down to hospital. The journey in the wagon would be far to bumpy, and it would only aggravate the spread of poison in your system.' His soft brown eyes held my gaze. 'You've got to promise me to be brave. Your big friends Ricky and George will be here soon to help. I have no freezing solution or anaesthetic of any kind. But I must not wait any longer. Now don't worry. Leave everything to me.'

By then, my leg was aching badly. But this, coupled with a grinding pain in my groin along with a high fever to boot, also meant that I didn't care much what he did.

I was becoming dizzier by the moment.

Time seemed to slow down. I felt increasingly hazy. Everything outside my body seemed far away. It was an awful feeling.

As the boys held me down, the doctor gave me a roll of bandage to bite on and began to cut. I shrieked as the knife sliced into the swollen skin. I felt the boys gripping me harder to hold me down. Tears gushed from my eyes as the blade bit further into the mass of inflamed flesh. Then whoosh . . . a stream of poison and pus spurted out.

The immediate relief was tremendous but shortlived.

The worst was to come. When it came the shock made me scream. One of the boys put the bandage roll back in my mouth while the rest used all their strength to hold me still while Doc inserted the drainage material into the wound and high up inside the leg to prevent the healing process from being too rapid. Clever this Doc. With the drain, he would now be able to tap this most potent of poisons every day until I was out of danger.

Apparently I fell asleep before the boys had let go of me, but afterwards George told me the Doc was pleased because I was as brave as an Austrian boy. Coming from the Doc, that was praise indeed.

What's more, his quick surgery resulted in steady improvement in my recovery from a bite that could have been fatal. But I had been lucky. According to Doc, had I had been bitten by the female of the species, I would have been pushing up daisies long before I'd even reached the ripe old age of thirteen.

12

Snakes and Silk

'Bergie, you can get up and go back to your own cabin today,' Doc announced cheerfully.

For two days, I had been pestering Doc to release me.

'Gee thanks Doc, I really do feel great.'

'So you might, but I want you to report back every morning for a check-up and be sure to take things easy. It'll be a few days yet before you're fully recovered.'

I hurriedly dressed and entered Doc's dispensary to say goodbye. This I found difficult. I was so grateful to this man who had saved my life that I could have hugged him. But I thought I was too grown up to show such affection — especially in front of my two best friends at Siwanoy, Whitey and Alec, who had come up the trail to meet me —

so I shook his hand.

★ ★ ★

It was the Night of the Big Gathering, where many troops sat down together in a giant circle for a night of entertainment. Fortunately there was no sign of rain, though the air was very humid.

Out beyond the glare of the camp fire, the twinkling stars and the dancing fireflies were unable to dispel the darkness.

That night, I was content, partly because I was back on my feet, and also because it was my turn to entertain the Circle. My rendition of the 'Old Kent Road' went down well. I remembered all the words and movements, even though it had been two years since Pete Gifford and I performed the same number in a show our orphanage presented on Broadway. The show was called Gratefully Yours. It was our way of saying thanks to the American actors and actresses for all their help in enabling our orphanage to come to America. It was also because of this show that I got to know two people who treated me with great kindness: Gertrude Lawrence and Paul Robeson.

★ ★ ★

At last came story-time. The tale was to be 'My Burning Feet', a scary tale told with great skill. Actually, it was a blend of two well-known legends from different hemispheres — the Abominable Snowman from the Himalayas and Bigfoot from the Rocky Mountains. Set in the Amazon jungle, the story was about a foolhardy boy named John who would not listen to his scoutmaster, and strode forth alone in the dead of night in search of the moaning and glowing that occurred from time to time in the jungle. The story ends with the discovery of John's scout belt buckle — all that remained of poor little Johnny. There is a moral to this story, of course, but I must confess I didn't pay much heed to its message at the time.

Our fire was burning low when one of the leaders quietly entered the middle of the circle, approached the Chief Scoutmaster and in whispers just loud enough for us to overhear, he said with a deliberately secretive air:

'Chief, we've just heard there are three dangerous maniacs on the loose. Apparently they escaped from the lunatic asylum and were last reported heading this way.'

'Thanks, Barney,' replied Chief. He then turned to us and spoke in a serious tone:

'Okay, you lads, I want you all to hit the sack now. The bugler will blow taps in fifteen minutes.'

I was more than happy to go to bed, as I was very tired.

Doc was right, I wasn't yet back to full strength. Thank goodness Mac was in our cabin. He was big and strong — a useful sort of guy to have around in case some looney visited us during the night.

I was determined not to go to sleep until taps was blown. I loved listening to taps. And that night, the line 'God Is Nigh' gave me extra comfort.

Actually, I didn't really believe the maniac message we had overheard, but I wasn't going to take any chances, so I said an extra prayer for our safety. Just in case.

★ ★ ★

In the deep quiet of night, I suddenly awakened with a start. In an instant, I was wide awake. I heard somebody running towards our cabin, perhaps not quite running, more like stumbling or lurching his way forward, but definitely heading in our direction.

As yet, I was not absolutely convinced there was a madman out there in the outer darkness, but whoever he was, he took ages to draw near the cabin, and then, thank goodness, he passed on by.

My relief was short-lived, however, for suddenly I heard a thump, followed by shouts and groans.

God Almighty! It must be one of the maniacs! There could be no other explanation.

It was only then I noticed the rain. Jeepers Creepers, I cried out to myself, they've murdered somebody in the pouring rain!

My imagination ran wild. Then I peered at the open door of our cabin and was petrified into complete immobility. There, framed in the doorway, stood a big black man with wide round glaring eyes, arms outstretched, his ham-like hands gripping the door frame. Clenched between his gleaming white teeth was a sheath knife with a blade long enough to skin a buffalo.

I tried to scream but not a sound escaped from my lips. It was then that I must have passed out with fright, for that was my last memory until I opened my eyes in the morning light.

'Holy cow, I'm alive!' I shouted and then told my friends the events of the previous night.

We all decided I'd had a terrible nightmare. Except Whitey. He reckoned my problem was a feverish relapse. Trust Whitey to think that one up.

The nightmare was later verified, however, when we learnt that one of the Scout leaders, slightly worse for drink, had stumbled over a guy rope and fallen heavily on the Scout-master's tent. Still, Whitey tried to convince everyone that I was still soft in the head from the spider.

★　★　★

Two days later, I raced down to the nature lodge looking for Alec Munroe. We had known each other for years, and both of us were now realising that our friendship, although calm and unassuming, was deep-rooted.

'Hi, Alec,' I said, 'I thought I would find you here. Do you remember that I promised I'd help you trap a live snake for your reptile badge? Well, how about coming with me now? We're bound to find a ribbon snake higher up on the reservation in this warm weather.'

Alec jumped at the chance. I had obtained my reptile badge the year before and was wrongly considered a bit of an expert. This year it was going to be Alec's turn.

Sometimes it could rain cats and dogs in these rolling Connecticut hills, But today, the sun sure shone brightly and promised to be hot.

'I'll tell you what, Alk. We'll get a couple of cokes and drop them in the devils bath tub, and drink them on the way back.'

We kept to the trails wherever possible. After all, it was rattlesnake country, to say nothing of poison ivy and poison oak. We rested at the foot of an old jack-pine and Alec filled me in on what happened while I was bedridden.

'Hey Alec, what happened after Ped got stung by the bee?' I interrupted.

'Oh, he's fine. Doc managed to get the sting out in one piece,' Alec replied reassuringly.

★   ★   ★

The previous Sunday morning when, having fallen in for church parade in full dress uniform, our Scoutmaster, C. T. Paul, called us to attention. At the same time, a bumble bee was causing some alarm among our line of boys. Ped was standing next to me when the busy bee saw fit to alight on his neckerchief.

'Don't move a muscle, Peter,' ordered C.T. 'I promise you the bee will not sting if you keep perfectly still.'

'Excuse me, chief', answered Whitey, 'I heard that if a bee has gorged itself on too much intoxicating nectar, it's liable to sting anything, sir, moving or not!'

I don't know if Whitey was correct, but everybody started laughing — except Ped — who stood motionless and expressionless.

Meanwhile, the bee walked around his neckerchief and then found a gap between neck and neckerchief. Out of the corner of my eye I could see Ped struggling to keep still.

'What the hell do I do now?' Ped said, exasperated.

'Keep still, Peter,' roared C.T.

'I can't, sir, the bloody thing is crawling down my back.'

Then it happened. Ped let out an ear-splitting yell and jumped two feet in the air as the bee stung him hard.

Even C.T. was bent double with mirth. By the time we arrived at our open air chapel, he had to appeal to us all. 'Please stop laughing.'

★ ★ ★

'Gosh, I wish I was staying with you for another fortnight, Bergie,' Alec sighed wistfully.

Hypnotised by the silence and tranquillity of these gorgeous foothills, I wanted to sit there forever.

'I wish you could too, Alk. Shoosh,' I whispered, pointing to a mound of coarse scrub. 'There's your snake Alec and he's a whopper. That's no ribbon. Gee whiz, it's a big grass snake and he hasn't seen us.'

Its colour glistened like polished stones. By my reckoning it's new unblemished skin could be no more than a day old. She was a beautiful sight.

I moved quickly. But my forked stick pinned the blighter to the ground just a fraction too low down from its head. Quick as I was, the snake was quicker. Its jaws clamped down across the palm of my hand and bit deep into the fleshy part by the ball of the thumb. The snake was four feet long, which made for a powerful and painful bite.

I had been bitten by a grass snake before, but not by one this size. Instinctively I forgot about the snake and attended to my hand which was bleeding slightly from the two tiny puncture marks though I knew from experience there was nothing to worry about.

'For crying out loud, Bergie,' Alec cried. 'In the space of a fortnight, you've been bitten by a poisonous spider, seen goddam madman in your delirium, and now you've been bitten by the biggest bloody snake I ever saw.'

'Yeah, but for God's sake, don't tell no one, leastways not before you're gone. Doc will be hopping mad if he gets to hear of this.'

The next day, the English boys were on their way home. I purposely kept out of their way though I was far from being lonely. Whitey was already ferreting me out. If anything, I felt as free at this moment as at any time that came to memory. Apparently unbeknown to me, because of the seriousness of my condition due to the wretched spider, the camp's chief scout had been in regular contact with Mr. Griffin, our superintendent. As a result of their conversations, I was granted an extra two weeks holiday.

'Hi Bergie, come on down the valley with me to the store, we'll git ourselves some clay pipes and drift off into the hills aways. Hank said he would come. He knows where there's a good corn field, where the silk is just about right to smoke.'

'You bet I will,' I said with enthusiasm.

'Hey, is that true, Bergie?'

'Is what true?'

'I heard you got bit by a big grass snake.'

'Whitey, how in tarnation do you get to know everything that goes on? Look.' I showed him my hand and the faint marks of a snake bite.

'Gee, that ain't much.'

'I know it isn't any great shakes,' I replied in a know-it-all voice, 'but you gotta remember that a snake's fangs are like needles. Just look and see how far apart the teeth marks are. It sure was a big one. Ain't that right Hank?'

'Yeah, good job it weren't an Eastern Back. You'd never have survived an Eastern Back rattler and a black widow. Come to think of it, you were dead lucky it was only the male of the species. They're only half the poison of the female.'

Hank wasn't his real name, but somehow it suited him, and from an early age the nickname stuck. He was a local boy from close by and although not a scout, he often called for his friend Whitey which is how I came to know him.

Hank was a typical American hillbilly, tall for his age, big-boned, lean and gangly. He could also ride a horse bareback. It was also Hank who showed us how to smoke the corn silk.

★　★　★

There was no way you could call the store a shop. Like every other building stuck out in the middle of nowhere, it was more of a log cabin except in this case it was half shack, half cabin. Yet inside, there was every conceivable item you could think of, and a lot more besides, most of it second hand.

The store was owned and managed by Jim. I reckon the business he received from Camp Siwanoy is what helped keep his head above water. Jim was all right, but he also moaned a lot about how he had to struggle night and day to make ends meet.

'Howdy, Jim, how's things today?' asked Hank.

'Not bad, Hank. Hi, Whitey, hi, Hugo.'

Jim was just about the only person who called me by my Christian name. He said it was because I was an English boy, though God knows why that should make any difference.

We purchased our clay pipes, a candy bar each and headed further up into the countryside.

Having filled our pipes, we sat down on the edge of the field and whiled away the sunny afternoon chatting, perfectly content with life and at peace with our surroundings.

I told Hank about my dream in the mountains.

He wasn't surprised. Taking an extra long puff on his clay pipe, he said: 'I'll mention your dream to my Pa. He knows these hills even better than I do. My Pa's got a lot of local history in him. I reckon he'll know the whereabouts of that burnt out cabin for sure. There aren't too many of them up at that height. Yep, that's a mighty interesting dream.'

By this time, I was coughing. So was Whitey. Smoking corn silk never bothered Hank though.

The summer shadows were lengthening, it was time to go. We said goodbye to Whitey's friend at the store, and slowly made our way back to Siwanoy, happy in the knowledge that there were more days to come like the one we just shared.

13

Two Islands

On arriving back at the Gould Foundation after the long Siwanoy holiday, my normally high spirits took a nose-dive, a condition grown-ups call the Monday blues. I think I was just home-sick for my mountains.

Still, I welcomed Ralph's suggestion to go and explore an expanse of water not far from our institution.

Although English, Ralph was from Ohio. His stay with us was brief, like many young evacuees. From time to time, they would appear, stay with us for a spell and then move on.

Perhaps I should have been more inquisitive over these comings and goings but I don't think one thinks of these things until one grows up a bit more. At least, I never did.

Ralph was older and bigger than me, dark-haired, dark-eyed, restless and fearless. He must have been a handful for his foster parents, back in Ohio. He had an insatiable appetite for dangerous adventure, which was possibly why he usually preferred his own company. But we got on well together and I liked him.

The temperature at noon was in the mid-eighties despite the fact that the long summer days were beginning to shorten.

It was Ralph who broke the silence.

'Let's swim out to that little island, Bergie, it looks uninhabited.'

'Heck Ralph, that's Goose Island and it's a shade too far for me to swim out there with my dodgy shoulder.'

The baseball season was coming to an end and my pitching arm had been painful lately. We had a good baseball team and called ourselves the British Lions, even though we always had at least two American boys in the team.

'How d'you know the name of the island?'

'I dunno, Ralph, I just heard tell some time.'

'Is it uninhabited?'

'So they say, I've never been there myself. Come to think of it, I don't know anyone who has. Everybody says its a dirty smelly old place, so someone's been there, that's for sure. Hey, wait a minute, I've just remembered. When I was going to school at P.S. 81, my Italian friend, he was called Ralph too, mentioned the island to me. He said nobody goes there 'cos it's horrible.'

'I vote we go and see for ourselves. The water will do your arm good. In any case, you've swam a darn sight further than from here to that pesky little island. I don't reckon its more than a quarter of a mile away.'

Ralph seemed to be surer of me than I was but I didn't want to appear scared.

'Okay, Ralph, you're on. Let's leave our gear here, I don't fancy walking round in wet clothes.'

The water was cold and far from clear, even though the whole bay was tidal. Just over half way, my arm started acting up and I was having difficulty raising it out of the water. Progress was slow and after about another hundred yards my shoulder didn't feel that it was part of me any longer.

'Ralph, my shoulder is cramping up,' I called to him. We both trod water while he managed to massage some warmth back into it. We then carried on swimming. With approximately two hundred yards to go, we repeated the process.

On wading up to firm ground I noticed how slimy and soft it felt under foot. But finally, we reached solid ground at last. We then looked round for a suitable spot to get back into the water and wash away the horrible stench and filthy black mud that clung to our legs. With my shoulder and arm aching, I was in no hurry to swim back.

'Never mind, Bergie, the tide will turn soon enough and we'll almost be able to walk back,' he joked.

The sun soon warmed us up and our spirits rose accordingly. Sitting down on the scrappy old beach with the satisfied feeling of achievement inside me, I recalled the other time I waited for an outgoing tide.

'Do you know what Ralph? There was another time I waited for the tide to turn.'

'What do you mean exactly?'

'Well, we were staying the night on Fire Island. That's way out on the Long Island Sound somewhere. C.T., our scoutmaster, was in charge of us. He's a good guy. Alec and I get invited sometimes in the winter to his house for the weekend. We have a great time . . . Where was I? We beached our row boat on the skinniest part of the island. That was C.T.'s brainwave 'cos it meant that we could see a stretch of water on both sides just by turning our heads from east to west.' I paused for a moment and thought how to carry on with my story.

'Are you still listening Ralph?'

'Yeah, go on. Just because I'm layin' down with my eyes closed taking in the sun don't mean I'm not listening.'

'Right. We were all settling down for the

night happy as Larry and looking forward to sleeping under the stars when a God Almighty storm kind of exploded right on top of us really quickly. One moment, all was quiet and peaceful, and then crash, bang, all hell broke loose. C.T. said the storm came in with the tide. We turned our boats upside down, dragged them together and rigged up as much shelter as we could, which was mighty little. Luckily it wasn't too cold, for our cover was next to useless. We were beginning to take a real hammering 'cos the rain was not only bucketing down but was almost horizontal because the wind was so strong and fierce. I remember C.T. saying the wind was coming straight at us from the South Atlantic and although he appeared calm outwardly, I could tell he was a mite worried because the water kept rising, and our island was slowly disappearing.'

Pausing once more in my story, I swatted a skeet that was bothering me.

'You know, Bergie, I'd swear you were a full-blown American the way you're relating your tale.'

'That's because I've just spent most of the summer with Hank and Whitey up at Siwanoy. Just give me another couple of weeks down here and I'll be back to speaking me normal mixed up English again. We spend half our time with English kids and the other half with Americans. It's no wonder we get all mixed up. Now where was I? Oh yeah. It was about two o'clock in the morning. We all had to get up and move everything further inland, not that anyone was asleep anyway. The water was nearly lapping our boots. Finally we placed ourselves nearly dead centre of the island. Fire Island is low, not many feet above sea level and near as flat as a pancake. I tell you Ralph, I've never seen such a storm, sheet and fork lightning followed by thunder rolling round and round, and the rain still coming slantwise down and across with enough force to sting summat awful. Then one time the lightning lit up the whole sky and we got the shock of our lives. All our part of the island for one instant was bathed in light, bright as day. A fantastic view.

'Trouble was there weren't much island left, about ten yards by my calculating and then darkness descended again. C.T. told us to make ready to depart in our boat, which we did in a jiffy and there we all stood, ready for the worst. I was able to smell the salt water, real strong. Even in the dark we could see it on both sides of us. The sound of the crashing waves mingled with the howling fury of the wind and rain. Yessiree, there we all were, standing there being battered and buffeted. But one thing was sure, C.T. wasn't going to launch the boat unless we felt the water under our feet. Nobody was looking forward to launching boats through those waves. They looked awful fearsome from where we were standing.'

'Did you feel excited, Bergie?' Ralph interrupted. This was probably the nearest adjective to 'frightened' in his vocabulary.

'Hell, no. I was right scared to tell you the truth. While I was standing there it reminded me of when I left Scotland on the Empress of Australia way back early in the war. Battle stations were called because the U-Boats were having a go at us. The whole crew were ready to abandon ship if it became necessary, but it didn't. Anyway, we watched the storm through the night and as the tide receded, the storm seemed to go with it and mercifully the island started growing again. Yep, that sure were some night, Ralph, you would have enjoyed it.'

'Gee whiz Bergie, that's what I call living.'

★ ★ ★

We started swatting the skeets more vigorously, but with the lowering of the sun, the mosquitoes were starting to zoom in on us with full force. Ralph reckoned they could

205

smell us. I didn't argue the point, though I didn't think they would have a nose big enough.

We had a choice to make, either we covered ourselves with that stinking mud to protect our naked bodies from the vicious mites, or we swam back to the mainland, got dressed and called it a day.

Ralph said the choice was mine, as he was concerned about my shoulder. I chose the former, mainly because I figured that the swim back would wash most of the mud off and that we would be clean enough to put our clothes back on. Plus we would have time to explore the island, and besides the tide had not quite reached its low point yet.

The skeets were a real nuisance, but plastering ourselves with the filthy black stuff eased our torture and enabled us to do what we had come to do. We must have resembled two aborigines exploring the island. Ralph reckoned a boomerang wouldn't be amiss in our hands. The actual exploration of the island didn't take more than half an hour, and it wasn't all that interesting.

'I guess we might as well get back,' I said.

Ralph agreed. Luckily my arm and shoulder held out and because the tide had turned earlier, the swimming distance was considerably less than on our way out.

On approaching the Foundation I said goodbye to Ralph, who lived in a different cottage and then came across George as he was about to leave.

George was a really nice guy, and was a great friend to my brother in the short time they knew each other. An Irish American boy from Fordham, he lived very near Christopher Columbus High School. That's where the older boys first met him. Over the years he had been a loyal friend to many of us.

It was Paddy, for that was his nickname, who had introduced me to ten pin bowling, not to bowl, but to earn some money as a Pin Boy. I was dead keen to earn a few bucks and C.T. had promised me that if I could scrape enough dollars together, next summer at Siwanoy I could go on the week-long pony trek deep into the Catskills.

I had gone with George to see the bowling alley boss.

'He's not very big, George,' he said. 'In fact, I think he's too small'

'Don't you believe it Alan, he's tough and fast. You try him out and I'll guarantee that within a week, he'll be the fastest pin boy you've got.'

'Okay, Sunny Jim, what do they call you?' Alan addressed me once more, and then added 'What hours do you want?'

'I can make five to eight most evenings, sir'

'Goddammit, that's a time I find easy to fill. Never mind, George says you're all right. That'll suit me, but mind you call me Alan, not this Sir malarkey.'

With such an incentive I soon became fast at the job, an essential requirement, and although I was still only five foot nothing, I could pick those pins up and stick them on their spikes as quickly as anyone. There was nothing automatic to aid a pin boy in those days. You sat on the edge and after the bowl had done its work, you jumped down quick and sorted the pins out. The faster you were, the better the customer liked it, and I picked up a good few dollars in tips.

One evening they were short a pin boy and the boss was telling one couple they would have to come back later.

'Please, Alan, if you put me down on lane three and four, I'll handle both lanes at once, and you won't have to turn your customer away.' I volunteered.

It wasn't bravado. I knew I could do it if I was willing to sweat a bit, and boy, did I sweat. For two and a half hours non-stop. Talk about shattered, but I collected twenty dollars including the tips that night. I was rich like I'd never been rich before. Unfortunately, Mr. Griffin soon limited my

208

hours because my schooling was beginning to suffer.

★ ★ ★

'Holy Moses, Bergie, if you could only see yourself in the mirror, you look as though you've been in an Irish peat bog. What a state you're in! Where in hell's name have you been?'

'Hi George, we've just arrived back from Goose Island. Ralph and I swam out there. I sure don't want to do it again.'

'Jeepers, I should hope not, it's a filthy place. No one goes there. Leastways not twice.'

'Yeah, I know that now. Still, it was summat to do.'

'Look Hugo, I'm glad I caught up with you. I've come to say goodbye. My draft papers have come through for the Army. I am going to try and get into the Parachute Regiment.'

'Suffering catfish! Jeez Paddy, I am sorry, I'm gonna miss you summat rotten.' I said goodbye to my friend and shook his hand. 'C'mon Paddy, I'll walk to the end of Stillwell Avenue with you and we can sing your favourite Irish ditty, that is if you can stand the sight and smell of me.'

'Sure thing, Bergie.' Then we broke into the sad little Irish song:

'Oh Paddy dear and did you hear
The news that's going around
The shamrock is forbid by law
To grow on Irish ground.
I was met by Mr McIntyre
And took him by the hand
And said how is Ireland?
And how does she stand.
He said she's the most
distressful country that you'll ever see
They're hanging all the Irish
For the wearing o'er the green.'

I watched him disappear around the corner before returning to the cottage, intending to have a nice hot soak. The bath had to wait a little longer though, while I answered a telephone call from C.T. who invited me to stay with friends of his in the Appalachians for the weekend. My spirits soared to heights unknown since my last days at Siwanoy.

14

Lost Weekend

As the months stretched on, my evacuee friends were disappearing from all around me. George had gone. And my brother Carol was on his way back to Blighty to join the British Navy. Even 17 year olds were welcome recruits.

The boys of my immediate age group, fourteen or thereabouts, were fast outgrowing me physically, and I was beginning to worry that there was something wrong with me though I learned to cope with this problem pretty well, with my love of sports and outdoor pursuits. I also had a mischievous Peter Pan outlook on life that kept me happy. Or so I'm told.

Nevertheless, with the ranks thinning all around me, I will always be grateful to C.T. Paul for the incredible weekend I spent with him and his chum who lived high up in the Green Mountains of Vermont. His friend was a wealthy man in more ways than one.

Arriving at our destination in the dark left me unaware of the sheer magnificence of the place, until the next morning, that is, when from my bedroom window I looked out over a valley flooded with golden light. In the distance, a shaft of sunlight pierced the dense green forest and struck the surface of a silvery lake. I couldn't believe my good fortune and vowed not to miss a minute of it.

Hurriedly I dressed and scampered downstairs to where C.T. and his friend were already tucking into breakfast — pancakes with maple syrup.

'Good morning C.T. Good morning, sir. That sure is a cracking view from my bedroom window.'

'Yes, my boy, and that trail in front of you goes right down to the lake. It is all my land and you're welcome to explore it. Don't get me wrong son, I don't mean that in a selfish way, C.T. will vouch for that. No-siree, this land is for preserving, at least while I'm alive and kicking.'

Prior to my coming downstairs, the two men had been discussing a rumour of a proposed road cutting through the valley to the next county. 'There'll be no city folk poking their noses in and spoiling things here,' my host said. 'City folk always spoil things. I should know, I was one myself once and was probably as guilty as the next man. However, I made money, lots of it, and I believe I put it to good use buying this valley. I like to think I'm doing my bit for posterity, in protecting some of God's green acres.'

'I promise you, sir, I'm no city boy, even though I have to live in the Bronx for a spate.'

'Heck I know that son. Listen, C.T. has told me how you love wilderness. After breakfast Rose will set you up a picnic. Then off you go, keeping to the trail mind. Oh, and before you hit the lake, call in on Red. He kinda looks after the outdoors for me. He talks a lot for an Indian but my advice is to hear him out. Wisdom just oozes out of the old fella. He is also a good story-teller. You can't miss the jasper, his pine lodge lays back off the trail aways, but still in sight of the lake. He loves his lake, perhaps more than any other part of his domain. I say his domain, because he is part of the valley like no-one else could ever be. Meanwhile Clarence and I have a lot to talk about. Mind you're back before dark 'cos dinners at sundown.'

★ ★ ★

The few clouds visible in the sky above were no threat to the sun as I threaded my way down the winding path, strolling mainly through jack-pine, thickened up here and there with oak, elm, chestnut and maples.

213

After a quarter of an hour I rounded a bend and saw the log cabin. Not sure of my next move, I paused to think of how to introduce myself. I need not have worried. Red suddenly materialised in front of me.

'Howdy boy, I heard you approaching some ways back, been sort of expecting you.'

'Hi, I'm staying up at the house for the weekend. I'm on my way to the lake, maybe go for a swim. I tried real hard to come down quiet like an Injun. Have you lived here long, sir?'

'My friends call me Red, so that can include you. In answer to your question, young'un, the answer is yes. I do move around some, anywhere there's hills and valleys, that's where I can live, but I base myself here. This is my home.'

'Cripes, that don't 'arf sound a good way to live. I tried walking to Texas once, but I didn't get very far, about fifteen miles I suppose.'

'That's none too long a trek for a fit young lad. What happened you never reached further?'

'We were running away, and a motorist tipped off the cops as we were hitch-hiking. Not that I mind now, because I'm having a good time of late, especially here.'

'Ah, I'm glad to hear it, son. But tell me, you're not from these parts, are you?'

'I know but, honest, I do feel I belong in the mountains. Some of the other kids don't understand how much I love being alone in them, but C.T. does.'

'So do I, boy, and that's good, but you gotta be careful afore taking off by yourself into unknown territory. Check out the local knowledge first. It could save you from a whole heap of trouble.'

'Thank you, Red, I'll bear that in mind.'

'Did you say bear that in mind? Son, you just reminded me of something that happened a long time ago. Sit down and stay apiece, it's an interesting story.'

Minutes later, we arrived at Red's cabin and sat down on the veranda. Red disappeared inside to fetch a few cans of root beer and then proceeded to hold me spellbound with his tale.

★   ★   ★

'Like you, my friend, I love the hills. So one day, having the itch for adventure, I wandered off my reservation and kept on going ever upwards. I just wanted to see what was over the next hill. Nothing unusual about that.

'Getting a mite tired, I lay down on my back, soaking up the sweetness of my surroundings. Time seemed to stand still as I fixed my gaze on a turkey buzzard way up in the blue. The day was hot and heavy, ideal for air currents. A buzzard loves air currents and is a master at using them. Sometimes he will float up there for hours with hardly a wing beat. The bird is sharp-eyed and possessed with infinite patience, yet despite his apparent laziness, he never goes hungry.

'Anyway, a thick mist enveloped my part of the mountain quite quickly, my fault for not observing the change in cloud direction. I got turned round a bit. A white man would say he was lost, but an Indian is never lost in the wild, just turned round on occasion.

'The dark fell down in a hurry that evening, on account of the low cloud. Generally the weather had been wet for a spell, so I headed for a thick clump of pine lower down. When it's damp, son, you will find that a goodly clump of jack-pine can still provide you with a dry bed for the night. Yep! Pine sure is a friendly wood.

'There were none too many persons populating the forests in them days, but I met one in that pine clump. He was roughly the age I am now, so you can see between the three of us, we stretch back a long ways. I think I'm correct in saying he was a young man when your George IV was King of England. Still, I'll try and tell you his story as he related it to me.

'There were no reservations then. Indians were free as the wind. Tribes tolerated each other as long as they didn't infringe on each other's liberties. All our peoples harmonised with the land, but no one owned any part of it. Ownership only came with the white man. The red man held sway over the land from the Atlantic to the Pacific and all that separated our mountain ranges, were rivers and forests. In the East we have the Catskills, Alleghenys, Adirondacks and many more. The Iroquois were the dominant nation hereabouts. This then was our time, the time of the red man, yet in this tale we talk of a boy about your own age, a warrior boy.'

The old man paused in his story. He took off his battered old hat and wiped his brow before replacing it. There were many pauses, Red was in no hurry. Little did I realise I would be listening to him for most of the day.

One time, when he brought his tale to a standstill, he reckoned that our thoughts were harmonised and were being recognised in the Spirit World and that the day would come long distant when we would meet again.

The sun was now pouring out the heat and we were downing our second root beer when the old man continued his story.

'The moon had shown it's full face

countless times when the boy took to wandering. He went off alone for long periods. His mother and father naturally worried when he was away. 'Where have you been all this time, my son?' The boy's reply was mostly the same, 'I've been watching the bears, Mother,' he answered. The boy and his father had many upsets over the months. Time and again the parents would say: 'It is too dangerous for you to watch the bears, and there are to be no more visits.' The boy would respond 'I must go father, I must go!' He was simply powerless to comply with his parents' request. Every time he came home, he would say, 'I am sorry father, I am sorry mother. I had to go.'

'The distraught father finally decided to share his problems with the village elders. A meeting was arranged to discuss the situation, and the decision they came to was a wise one.

'The boy was marked by the bear's spirit, and in future he was to be known as Little Bear. His excursions into Bear country were not only to be tolerated, he was to go with the blessings of the elders.

'As the moons waxed and waned, Little Bear's wanderings became more frequent and of longer duration. Now, when he arrived home from his rovings, instead of saying, 'I was watching the bears,' he would say, 'I have been with my bears.' The elders in the tribe treated him with respect, young as he was. The Great spirit is watching over the boy, they whispered. He is destined to become a great warrior.

'At this time, there was some feuding between villages and sadly, as often happens, anger and stupidity filled many hearts. One dawn, a large neighbouring war party raided Little Bear's encampment, resulting in blood being shed and the kidnapping of two young maidens.

'A few days after the battle, Little Bear returned to his village to discover his whole tribe had been called together. The Elders were in the process of forming a war party to seek revenge on their neighbours. Little Bear faced the whole tribe and advised them not to go to war. 'I will bring back our sisters, for they are our people,' Little Bear vowed. Such was his power and authority he carried all before him but one. The tribe's medicine man, jealous of the boy's popularity, stood up before the people of the tribe and accused the boy of pretending to see the bears all the time. Perhaps he said, he was visiting our enemies. Was he not away when the enemy came and stole our young brothers and sisters, and killed many of our warriors? Was he not away when his family needed him?

219

How did our enemies slip through our sentries to surprise us all so easily? Where was Little Bear in our time of need?

'The boy's father rose, terrible anger showing in his face, but his son restrained him, and requested of the elders permission to speak in his own defence.

' 'Many of you know I smell of bear. I eat with the bears, I sleep with the bears, and I pray to the Great Spirit with bears,' Little Bear said. 'If you go to war, our tribe will perish, and we shall be no more. The enemy's numbers are as countless as the leaves on many trees. We shall vanish with the wind. And you, Medicine Man, listen to my words. I will honour you as befits your station, but speak any more with forked tongue or you shall know the terrible power of the bear.' The sheer presence and personality of the boy produced a profound silence, and the medicine man sat down defeated.'

The old man sighed, his eyes focused on the past. I felt the thrill of the tale as he continued to unfurl it.

'Little Bear rose at dawn and made ready to depart. Three hands of summers had passed since he first saw the light of day, and though yet not a man, he possessed formidable strength of character. Coupled with his friendship and knowledge of the bear, the young warrior was ready. He said goodbye to his family and set forth on his journey.

'By the fourth night, the enemy feeling safe, camped unwisely between a fast running river and a forest edge. The maidens were still untouched and would remain so until the war party delivered them safely to their tribe. The fate of the girls would then be in the hands of the tribal council. As the big war party were far less anxious than previous nights, their camp fire was a little larger than usual. The scouts reported that there was no signs of enemy pursuit but there was an uncommonly large number of bears in the vicinity.

'Suddenly, a terrible sound rent the night air and blood-curdling roars echoed all around the forest edge, reverberating back and forth. Coming towards them was a huge male bear and straddled on the magnificent beast's back, a young warrior sat bolt upright. Never had the like been seen before or since. The war party stood motionless, mesmerised with the vision before them.

'Little Bear raised his arm. Then, in a voice of unchallengeable authority, commanded the war party to heed his words. The sight near froze their blood, for before their eyes, silhouetted by the fire light were more bears than all of the kidnappers had seen in their collective lifetime. The braves clustered together, fearful and full of anguish. The boy then continued speaking to his captivated audience: 'You must escort the maidens back to their rightful village. Your tribe must smoke the Pipe of Peace. There shall be no more bloodshed between our villages. If you fail to do as I command, my bears will destroy your whole tribe. Tell all your people that Little Bear has communed with the Great Spirit, and his word must be obeyed!'

'Little Bear then bent down and whispered to his brother, whereupon the huge bear turned and disappeared back into the forest, and once again the woods echoed to the mighty roar of many bears'.

★ ★ ★

'Gosh Red, that's the best story I've heard yet. I bet they took the gals back.'

The old man laughed. 'They sure did, son, but though that's the end of the tale, the mystery still remains. Little Bear was never seen again. His mother and father said the lad went North, even as far as the Great Divide. I asked the Sage that very same question and I'll give you the answer he gave me. Little Bear went to the land of Long Winters with his bears to save them from a terrible enemy who would soon arrive on our shores.'

'Cor, that can't all be true, surely,' I said, amazed.

'I've related to you exactly as told to me by the Sage. I reckon most legends have some truth. I am often sceptical about myths, as they generally go back so far that no one knows for certain of their origin. But if you want my honest opinion, this story has more than a mite of truth in it, and I'll tell you why. To be a Sage, you have to be a truthful man, and to be a wise man, you have to have truth in your heart, so you see son, the man that told me the story was kinda' special and had a heap of knowledge. And what you have to remember, son, is our folk law is passed down through the ages from sage to sage.'

★ ★ ★

'Gee, it sure beats all. Well, thanks again, Red. I'm going down to the lake now.'

'You do that, son, but keep to the trail. The forest verges are thick with poison ivy and poison oak. You're not dressed for the interior.'

'Okay, so long,' I shouted back as I again headed for the lake.

Standing by the water's edge, I looked out on the huge expanse of the land-locked body of water. Boy, it's big. I thought. There is no way I could ever swim across this lot. So far, my experience of lakes had been that they are both cold and murky. This one was certainly cold, but clearer than any I had come across before. It took me approximately five seconds to slip out of my shorts and singlet before diving off the jetty's edge. At this moment I was as close to the kind and gentle side of Mother Nature that any boy can get. Here I was alone in a vast wilderness, on a day where our big warm sun could only smile. Having finished my solitary swim, I hurriedly dressed and ate the lunch that Rose had kindly packed for me hours ago.

★ ★ ★

Then, all at once, like a thief in the night, a large heavy grey cloud appeared over the summit of the mountain to my left. A cool wind blowing gently from the lake heralded a summer storm. The sun now lower in the western sky, still shone brightly. I could see that the cloud may miss the sun, but the rain was falling on the other side of the lake, drawing ever nearer to where I was sitting.

I stood up, transfixed and motionless, unable to take my eyes off an unforgettable picture. The warm summer rain advancing across the lake gathered speed as the freaky dark cloud, now directly above me, shed millions of crystal clear raindrops which seemed to bounce off the surface of the lake. The brilliance of the sun, still shining, transformed the rebounded droplets into fiery jewels that danced for a split-second then dropped anonymously into the lake once more. As if this magnificent sight was not enough, this dazzling movement was framed by a rainbow so vivid I gasped at this celestial vision. No one who saw what I saw this day could ever forget the sight.

Soon, however, the cloud sped by and the sky cleared. I had to tell C.T. As I rushed back up the trail, I almost collided with Red. His leathery old face creased in a huge smile.

'Son, I can see you saw the storm come across the lake.'

'Yes sir, I sure did,' I stammered breathlessly.

As I said goodbye to this wise and simple man, I will never ever forget his parting words: 'Treasure the vision my boy, for it is a rare and beautiful sight granted to few people.'

15

Last Days at the Foundation

Participating in ball games was always an enjoyable part of my life. No matter what size or shape the ball, or whatever the sport, a ball seemed a natural part of me. Indeed you could say I was a 'Jack of all Balls and Master of None'.

However, learning to play the piano was always an unenjoyable part of my life, despite the fact that I came from a musical background. In the 1920s, before tuberculosis took my mother from this world, my parents were up and coming opera singers with the Sadler's Wells Opera House. I was told my mother was an accomplished pianist as well.

Apparently, I did not inherit her gift. Although Miss Montgomery, our music teacher, tried very hard to teach me to read music and play the piano, I was a hopeless case.

The final reckoning came one fine sunny day in the middle of a music lesson. In one ear, I heard excited voices of children playing basketball outside the window. In the other ear was the relentless ticking of the metronome demanding that I concentrate on my timing.

It was all too much for me. The call of the ball won. Before Miss Montgomery had time to gasp, I was out of my seat and head first through the wide open window and off to join the other boys.

My guilt notwithstanding, I felt compelled to pursue what I loved, and leave behind what I intensely disliked.

The subject of music lessons was never brought up again.

★ ★ ★

The main sports fields were a few hundred yards further down the road, but our back yard was large enough to cope with half a basketball court, which was all we needed for a full-blown match. While playing this particular game of basketball, it dawned on me that although the other guys, Alk, Tim, Jay, Klaus and Claud were younger than me, they were physically my equals. The realisation that I still had the body of a twelve year-old while all my friends and colleagues of my own age were well into adolescence, worried me.

As the months passed I became more and

more miserable, an alien state for me. Ironically, it was the forgiving Miss Montgomery who first noticed the depths of my unhappiness. One evening after supper she bade me report to her room, whereupon I poured out all my troubles to her. I then listened and learned.

She showed me that it was not the end of the world when I lost a fight (because just lately I had lost a couple). She also taught me that patience was a virtue and that I would grow up in God's own time. And perhaps above all, Monty made me realise that if you did your best, you never ever lost, whatever the outcome, a philosophy I carry with me to this day.

Miss Montgomery was a gem. When I finally left her room that day, my normally high spirits returned and during the rest of my stay in America, I never became that low again.

★ ★ ★

A week later, I was summoned to Mr. Griffin's office.

'Hello Hugo, how are you?'

'I'm fine, sir, thanks.'

'Good. Sit down please.'

'I hear you have been going through a

rough patch lately.'

'That's true, sir, I was, but I'm okay now thanks to Monty, oops I mean Miss Montgomery, sir.'

Mr Griffin smiled and continued:

'Yes, she is a brick and, incidentally, Hugo, she has a soft spot for you if I'm not mistaken. Anyway, Hugo, in view of your Peter Pan appearance, we would like to get you checked out. Now, don't get me wrong, we are not worried for your health or anything else for that matter. As you know, Peter Gifford is small in stature and is training to be a jockey at the Belmont racetrack.'

'Yes, sir' I said, too shy to mention that at least his voice had broken and he had hair under his arms.

'You went to see him a little while ago.'

'That's right, sir'

'How was he?'

'Just fine, Mr Griffin. I had breakfast with him and the other jockeys. I sure had a good time. I even climbed up on a great big white horse, but the darned beast kept rearing up on two legs. To be honest, sir, I didn't fancy those capers, it were kinda scary, but I didn't fall off.'

'Hm, good for you. Now then Hugo, I have arranged for you to stay in the city overnight, while our doctor carries out a few tests. Mrs Sperring will collect you in the morning. Is this arrangement agreeable with you?'

'I guess so,' I said, wondering what was in store for me.

★ ★ ★

The next day came round soon enough. 'Hi Hugo, all ready to go, are you? Say, can I trust you in the front of the car with me?'

'Yes, Miss Sperring, you can,' I smiled, sheepishly. 'I hope I'm a little more responsible than our last ride together.'

The last time I was in Miss Sperring's car, the other kids dared me to put my foot down on the accelerator as she drove us all along the Parkway. I could only just reach the pedal, but press it I did and the Oldsmobile surged forward rapidly. Boy, was she mad. Instantly slamming on the brakes she turned on me angrily, her lovely blue eyes flashing like fiery sapphires, and called us all a bunch of flatheads. I think that meant we were all at least one level lower than stupid. The good lady called us a lot of other things as well. In fact we all received a good verbal roasting, which in my naivety I did not think possible from such a beautiful lady.

In the hospital, they asked me what I thought were a lot of stupid questions such as, 'Do I like girls?' and 'Did I dream about them?' or 'Do I like chasing and catching them?'

'I prefer to go chasing round a baseball diamond or a football field,' I replied truthfully.

Then I was weighed, measured, an armful of blood was extracted and God knows what else. Feeling suddenly like an experimental guinea pig, I blurted out: 'Can I go home please?'

Absolute silence. To my astonishment, the doctor in charge granted me permission, and after assuring me that I was in tiptop condition and would eventually grow.

On my return to the Foundation, I learned that a tragic incident had occurred in my absence. No one saw the accident, but I heard that two American boys were playing near the overhead electric cables that served the Subway network, when the younger one slipped. The older boy, in attempting to rescue his little friend, reached out and managed to catch the lad, but precisely at that moment, the little fella had grasped the live wire in an instinctive effort to save himself from falling onto the track below.

Both boys died instantly.

Only a week previous to this tragedy I had climbed up onto the very ledge where those poor kids met their untimely end and rescued a pet rabbit that belonged to one of the younger kids in our cottage. Many times in the past I had sat up there, despite the fact that the area was out of bounds. Nevertheless, the death of those two kids affected me deeply. I never visited the ledge again.

★　★　★

It was about this time, I had a crush on one of our own girls. It was a secret that I kept locked up inside of me for most of my life. I only mention the fact because I am sure a lot of young boys and girls felt as I did, the pain and anguish of wanting to declare their calf love for the opposite sex, but were too shy to declare themselves. Her name was Ursula. She had a boyfriend who was older and far more mature than I was. This fact alone banished all thoughts of progress in this department. However, she was the very first girl I enjoyed looking at in a swim suit. Was this the moment? Was I at last slowly creeping towards adolescence?

★　★　★

It was December 1944. Christmas had come round once more and I was fortunate enough to be able to spend the whole of it with my friends the Fleming family in Long Island. I have never forgotten them.

Often their son Peter and I would nip down to the corner drugstore in the evening to meet the rest of his pals, girls as well as boys. It was all so natural for him mixing with girls, a pastime that was alien to the way I had been living.

At first, I was scared stiff of them, but they made me feel so welcome that I soon overcame my shyness. Everybody wanted to hear my English accent. Monty once told me that I had lost it altogether. To keep my friends happy, I used the only two dialects I knew — a posh Kings English and a version of the London cockney. I had to admit though, it was getting difficult these days because I mingled as much with Americans as I did the English. Luckily, my version of the Old Kent Road always kept them happy.

Yes, my time spent with the Fleming family was a welcome interlude into a way of life that was far less aggressive than what I experienced in the Bronx. I guess the Fleming family would be categorised as middle-class America. They had a lovely home filled with all sorts of luxurious items, such as big soft armchairs, beautiful curtains, deep piled carpets, and what's more in the kitchen, apart from the usual electrical appliances, they even had a dishwasher. Oh boy, could I have saved some time over the years with one of them.

The house was situated in a spacious tree-lined avenue, adjoining more of the same. Mr. Fleming was a bank manager, slim, dapper and very kind. His wife, a lovely warm woman, was as tall as him, but more generously proportioned. Some evenings we would saunter down to the corner drug store, meet up with Peter's pals, and commandeer the juke box for an hour or two. At other times, we would visit his friends' houses and play basket ball, or poker, or generally 'just mess around'.

★   ★   ★

Still, I am very grateful to all those people in the Bronx. They gave us a home, and as a local population, I had never experienced such generosity as they bestowed upon us British evacuees. Indeed it is fair to say that I suffered far more bad times with English kids than I ever did with Americans. That is partly due, of course, to the nature of institutional life.

Like all good holidays, they are soon over. Back at the Gould Foundation, life was not quite the same either. More and more of the older guys were leaving. My brother had long gone. He had joined the navy and was serving somewhere in the Atlantic on board *HMS Ajax*. One or two lads had joined the American forces as the United States was well and truly embroiled in the war by this time.

Occasionally word came through of another casualty due to the war. The first one I heard about was way back in 1942. Paul Bantock was shot clean out of the sky. He was just twenty one years old. On hearing this tragic news, his brother Granville went back to England and eventually joined the British Army.

The war was now going well for the Allies and we were informed that it would be over in 'the not too distant future'. A bland statement that I always regarded with scepticism.

About this time, I had to report to our own hospital for a course of injections, the theory being that they would speed up my growth. This was the result of those wretched tests I underwent two months earlier. Nurse was to administer them on my backside. I won't forget my first injection in a hurry, for it took me completely by surprise.

'Yeeowee! Hot diggety dog, nurse, that don't 'arf hurt, almost as much as when I used to get caned in the old days.'

'Yes, my lad, I've heard about these beatings you boys had back in the old country.'

'That's right, nurse, I've had a good few canings in my time.'

The nurse laughed heartily. 'I expect you deserved them.'

'Well yes, I suppose I did most of them, but in the old days at Langley Hall there was an old man we called Pa. He enjoyed whacking boys on their bare bums.'

The nurse was now laughing so loud she attracted the other two nurses' attention. 'Do you know what?' I continued, relishing the fact that I now had a live audience of four. 'There was one boy called Roy who he picked on in particular. Roy missed out on coming over here, cos he was born too early. Pa only had to see the poor bloke and if he was in hearing distance, he'd call him over and give him a good hiding, whether he had done anything wrong or not. Yep, poor old Roy used to skulk around in fear of his life.'

'Go on, Hugo! I'm sure you're exaggerating, or at least stretching the truth beyond the bounds of a good Christian soul.'

'It's the truth, I swear. It's funny isn't it, how some boys get picked on more than others. Take Mr Green, for instance. He was our last headmaster before we sailed over here. He never caned me but the other two headmasters, Old Birdnest and Old Ruggles, did. Roy was once collared by Old Ruggles. He told me that he must have been seen pinching some fruit from the kitchen gardens. We were always hungry in those days. Anyway, Old Ruggles got to hear of it somehow. We reckoned that he used some of the girls to spy on us from time to time, however I'm not certain if that was the case or not. What I do know for sure, 'cos Roy told me and crossed his heart, is that Old Ruggles approached him and marched him off to his study. On the way, he saw another boy by the name of Inky on account he was darker than the rest of us, and he said to him, 'Now son, I want to show you what I do with thieves,' and thereupon gave poor old Roy one hell of a licking.'

'Go on Hugo, you're sprucing again.'

'Scout's honour, it's the truth.'

'Oh I guess I believe you Hugo, but what happened to Roy?'

'I don't know, Ma'am. He didn't come with us to America. He was a fraction too old by the time war broke out. Shall I tell you about some more canings?'

'No, my lad, we've heard enough of you for one day. Off you go now. One thing though, the cane hasn't done you any harm, but thank goodness it has never been introduced here.'

'Ma'am, I would not let anybody cane me any more. I had my last beating at Silverlands. Do you want . . . ?'

'Goodbye, Hugo.'

Later on I was informed I had to undergo a further course of these injections. I wasn't too happy about them and I got the feeling Nurse didn't like the idea either.

A few days later, as I was running down the hill towards our hospital for another of those infernal jabs, the tapping in my head started again. This peculiar state of affairs had me worried lately, so I decided to have another chat with the nurse.

'Hi, Mary.'

'Don't be cheeky son, you best call me Nurse' she said with a twinkle in her eye.

'Nurse, just lately when I run I get this tapping sound in my head.'

'Hugo, you're impossible,' her face showing real consternation as she spoke.

'Honest to God, Nurse, I promise you it kinda worries me a bit. You don't think it's anything to do with these damned injections, do you?'

'I don't. It's more like you have a screw loose.'

'Funny you say that, Nurse. Can I tell you what happened to me way back even before my orphanage days? I remember it real clear 'cos it scared the living daylights out of me, and everyone else for that matter. It was even more frightening than when I lost the end of a pencil up my nose.'

Nurse sighed with an air of resignation, 'I'm sure there will be no peace in here until you've told me.'

'Well Nurse, it was like this. It was not many days after the bust up between Matron and her assistant over little Tony, who was only three, (my brother told me I was five at the time) but I remember it as though it were yesterday. We were all lined up at one end of the long garden for a running race. The winner was the one who touched the wire fence at the house end first. Oh, by the way, the hostel was in London. Anyway, those big houses all had basements with big stone steps leading up to ground level. The wire fence must have been very weak in the part I hit, because I just went straight through and landed head first — Bang! Boy did I scream as I contacted the bottom step. What I am trying to say Nurse, do you think I've got delayed action or something with this tapping?'

'Oh Hugo, oh dear. What am I going to do with you? Lord knows what you will come out with next. Be off with you now. Look, there's big Nick, go and plague the life out of him for a change.'

'Okay, Nurse, I'm gone, but if this tapping persists I'm coming back to have another moan.'

★ ★ ★

Big Nick was our head gardener. He was an Italian American and I often had little chats with him. Today, however, was not going to be one of them. I thought, if I play my cards right I could nip back to the cottage, grab a bite to eat and then sneak off to the bowling alley for a couple of hours Pin Boy duty.

The Easter term was drawing to a close and I was looking forward to a few days holiday with my friends in Long Island, when I received a message to go and see Mr Griffin.

After the usual formalities, came the bombshell.

'Hugo, the A.O. authorities have been in correspondence with us regarding the future of the boys and girls we still have left in our care.' Mr Griffin stopped speaking and shifted one or two papers about on his desk, and then without looking at me, carried on speaking. 'You of course, are one of the oldest still with us, and the time has come when we must discuss your future.'

'I don't know what to say, sir,' I said, taken aback.

'Don't say anything yet, just hear me out.' Mr Griffin was able to look at me now as he carried on talking. 'The war in Europe will soon end, possibly within a month or two. The time has come, Hugo, for you to make some decisions. The main one is whether to go back to England or to stay here with a view to becoming an American citizen. If you stay with us, you will be our responsibility until you're eighteen. If, however, you go back to England, then the Actors' Orphanage will be responsible for you once more. Either way Hugo, playtime is over for you, Peter Pan has had his day and growing up must now take precedence.

Oh Lord, I thought, I could do without this. These last twelve months had been great. I hadn't realised how happy I was.

It wasn't easy for Mr Griffin to convey this message. He knew I had to make a difficult decision.

For the next few days and nights my mind was in a turmoil. All the bad times were forgotten. My memories were now tuned in to all the happy occasions over the last five years, and there were many of them.

With a frightening abruptness I was forced to face up to a few realities. My childhood was slipping away and I didn't like it, not one little bit. Mr Griffin was right, at fifteen years of age I could no longer be Peter Pan.

I walked out of his office in a daze. I had never felt so insecure. Arguments for and against were numerous and compelling. I felt American, I spoke American and my best friends were American. If I went back to England, where would I go? Then again, if I stayed, what would I do? If I knuckled down at school, Mr Griffin said there was a good chance I could earn a place at Columbia University and take on a sports degree. I also knew that if I reported back to Mr Griffin and said, 'Please let me stay,' he would see to it that I could.

But what about my father? (What was he doing during the war?) Here was a man of my own flesh and blood. A man whom I hardly knew. I desperately wanted to stay, and yet all this time I had this dreadful feeling, it was my duty to go back and get to know my father.

Past events kept surfacing in my mind. My

nights were fitful and full of lingering doubts that led to many sleepless hours. Finally, the thought of not seeing my father again was the deciding factor. Consequently I told Mr Griffin. I would go back to England. I purposely did not say 'home', because I didn't know where that was.

Having made a decision I felt a lot better. My immediate future was now in forward motion.

In a matter of weeks I was on my way to Boston where I stayed the night in the Hotel Statler. (Forty years later, I was to spend another night at the same hotel, prior to running in the Boston Marathon.)

The very next day, with mixed feelings, I boarded the British Navy cruiser, the *HMS Sheffield*.'

16

Back to Blighty

I was, three days out from Boston, aboard the *HMS Sheffield*, a fighting cruiser of some distinction. Months earlier, she had limped into the harbour in a war-torn state and undergone a complete refit. Now, once again she was sea-worthy and nosing her way eastwards through the rolling, turbulent waves of the mid-Atlantic.

★ ★ ★

'Hugo, I hear on the wireless the Germans have surrendered.' said Hans in his usual charming way.

'Perhaps you get better more quick, yes?' Although his command of English was good, when one or two Dutch influences infiltrated into his speech, it was also quite amusing. Not that mine was much better, half English and half American! 'You be happy more now, yes, like me,' he continued.

My new friend Hans was very happy. He was at last going home to Holland. In the meantime, however, he had volunteered to look after me.

★ ★ ★

I must be the world's most wretched sea-going traveller. I won't say sailor as I don't want to insult them. At that moment, I'm ashamed to admit, I couldn't have cared less about the Japs or the Germans because, for the second time in my young life, I was too ill to care about anything.

Here, below decks, I was probably the most miserable boy on earth, lying in the hammock that Hans had slung between a couple of stanchions.

He was also worried about me. I hadn't eaten anything for seventy-two hours. Sea-sickness this intense is not only horrible; it's also rare. It turned out, I was the worst case he had seen in all his twenty-five years at sea. At least, that's what I overheard him say.

For his sake I drank a few sips of water, which I immediately vomited up again, and then pretended to nibble a dry biscuit. These, at least, had no weevils or maggots, like in the days of old, when ships sailed the seven seas for months on end.

Buck up, Bergie, and be thankful for small mercies, I told myself. If I'd been a sailor in those far off days, I might have been given up for dead and slung overboard.

Lying back in my hammock, I tried to forget the revolting stench that exuded from the engines and galley and the ceaseless heaving. Even now, I can recall shutting my eyes tightly and forcing myself to think of people I would never see again.

There was Ralph Fratiani, the Italian-American who befriended me in my first days in P.S. 81, the guy that taught me how to survive alone in the Bronx, and travel safely on the New York subway.

And Whitey and Hank, two American boys I would surely miss. Ironically, the only English boy I was really going to miss was Alec Munroe. Alec chose to stay in the States and become an American citizen. From what I could gather, he had less reason to return to England than I did.

Then there was dear old Monty. Miss Montgomery was one dedicated teacher, and I had a lot of respect for her.

I also thought of all the actors and actresses who had visited the Gould Foundation over the years. Lynn Fontaine and her sister Joan, Carry Grant, Douglas Fairbanks Junior ... My mind flitted over most of them, because like a ship that passes by in the night, my time with them was fleeting. Though fame and fortune in the theatrical world never meant much to me, there were two people I will never forget.

Gertrude Lawrence was a really sweet lady. I wonder why she invited me to see her occasionally. I bet my music teacher, bless her, was involved in arranging that. There was one time when I had the best seat in the house at one of the leading theatres on Broadway when Miss Lawrence was playing the lead role in Lady in the Dark. After the show, she took me out to dinner with some of her friends at the 400 Club. I must admit, I felt quite important sitting next to her.

The other was Paul Robeson. Now there was a big man in every sense of the word. So was his chauffeur Joe, who on several occasions collected me in a huge limousine to take me to Mr. Robeson's house. I guess Joe was pretty highly regarded because besides driving Mr Robeson around, he was also his friend and bodyguard.

One afternoon, he took me to a baseball game between the New York Yankees and the Brooklyn Dodgers. Never had I seen so many mad people in one place, shouting and screaming, not only at the umpires and players, but also at each other. While the game was thrilling, the crowds were definitely not my cup of tea.

Even now, I can see Paul Robeson in his flowing robes playing Othello with Gertrude Lawrence as the leading lady. Yessiree, they were two mighty good people.

And what about the Fleming family? I thought, drifting in and out of sleep. Okay, so they weren't famous, but apart from my time at Siwanoy, the holidays I had with them were among the happiest days of my life.

And then there was . . . Crikey, Bergie! I thought, maybe you're making the biggest mistake of your life by going back to England.

'Hello, Hans, have I been asleep?'

'Yes. It is good you sleep, but better for now you drink. Your body, it dry up without water. Tomorrow if no better you move to sick bay, the MO says doctor's orders.'

'I don't know about a dry body, Hans, but stepping on some dry land would help.'

★ ★ ★

Soon I was back into my hammock, shut my eyes and once again lost myself in the years gone by. Sandwiched between clean white sheets, tired and weak, I once more drifted into semi-consciousness, and my memories became even more vivid as the days slipped by, one into the next.

When I finally surfaced from my stupor, I

pondered my whereabouts. Oh yes, I was in sick bay, not that the transition had made any difference. I still felt bloody awful.

The MO popped his head round the corner, 'Ah Hugo, you're awake at last.'

I didn't tell him that I'd been awake ages, and that it just seemed easier to keep my eyes shut rather than watching the up and down motion of the wretched cruiser coping with the heavy Atlantic swell. Still, Hans had said we were more than halfway home.

The word 'home' knocked me sideways. Holy mackerel, where the hell is home? I thought.

'Hugo, you haven't even had a drink, it's just not good enough,' the MO chided.

I could see he was annoyed and so to placate his justified irritation, I downed half a glass of water. What the hell, I was thirsty anyway.

'Hans is coming shortly', he continued matter-of-factly. 'And being that the war with Germany is more or less over, the chief has given him some extra time off to be with you. After all, it's not every day we have such a young VIP among us,' he said sarcastically.

I was fast going off this guy. 'Excuse me Sir, what do you mean by more or less?'

'Well, officially over is correct, but it's very probable that one or two U-boat skippers under radio silence may still be unaware of the latest developments. That's why we are still under blackout regulations and on full alert.'

'Hi Hans,' I whispered, as the grey-haired crew cut solid-looking, friendly faced man entered my quarters. 'I've just drunk half a glass of water and do you know what, it's still inside me.'

'That is very good Hugo, you soon get better now.'

In the few days I had known Hans we had become good mates. He had a son about my age, who he hadn't seen since the outbreak of hostilities. He never talked about the early days of the war, but he sure had seen a heck of a lot of action. He did tell me about his younger days though. They were mainly good times for him.

'The sea is in my blood Hugo,' he once told me.

'I'll stick to Terra-Firma, thank you,' I thought.

From the first day Hans had drawn breath in his native coastal village, he was destined to sail the seven seas with the Dutch Navy. Not unlike my brother Carol who had had his own taste of naval excitement. In 1942, a captured German frigate was his mode of transport back to England. After the frigates conversion to a cargo vessel, a Dutch crew was assigned to her. So much merchant navy tonnage had ended in Davy Jones's locker, that it became necessary to convert many types of unlikely craft to carry goods.

Almost 17 years old, Carol, the only civilian aboard, could not have been in better hands. The voyage had also proven to be an interesting introduction to his naval career which commenced the following year.

During this period of the war, German submarines were very active off the North American coastline and it was considered far safer for cargo ships to cross the Atlantic under escort — this no doubt being the reason why the converted frigate was ordered to rendezvous with a convoy and proceed under the protection of two destroyers belonging to the Royal Navy.

For his part, the Dutch skipper was none too happy about joining up with such a large cargo carrying convoy. He felt he had a far better chance on his own. He was in command of a souped-up sailing vessel that could outpace any U-boat afloat, and therefore would have much preferred to rely on his own wits and experience.

Twenty four hours later, the weather changed for the worse and although the wind had not yet reached gale force, life was unpleasant for all those above deck. Not the best moment for the pandemonium that was to follow.

Radar equipment had detected the presence of enemy submarines. Carol's boat with her Dutch crew, was second to last in line. The nearest destroyer was some good way forward on the starboard side when the torpedo smashed into tail-end Charlie. Having just recovered from his almost sleepless night, my brother heard a muffled explosion and being that he had no duties to perform, he was able to view the sequence of events now unfolding before his eyes.

The last cargo ship in line had been struck amidships. A plume of black smoke belched forth, trailing upwards and gradually thinning in the turbulence of the low cloud cover above. A sorry sight no wartime sailor ever forgets.

The nearest destroyer swung around and, like a mother hen, raced towards her stricken chick, her bows knifing and crashing through the unfriendly waves. The cargo ship mortally wounded, floundered and wallowed helplessly in an effort to keep afloat. All to no avail. The gaping hole in the ship's heart meant its death throes were brief yet relentless. As the sea poured into her bowels, my brother witnessed a merchant ship quietly disappear from view, sinking beneath the angry waves tilting inevitably downwards to the ocean floor.

His young eyes, filled with sadness, he turned towards the destroyer, now hell bent on revenge. Perhaps a terrible anger had infected its crew.

The rearguard action that ensued was of a speedy ship o' war hurling depth charges in a seemingly haphazard fashion towards an unseen force. Whether by luck or good judgement, one or more of the deadly canisters found their target. And while many men, some with tears in their eyes, watched their dying comrades consumed by fire and water, they also cheered the demise of their opponents.

The Dutch skipper, fearing that his own ship was now in jeopardy, gave orders to head north at full speed. No invisible enemy was going to endanger his ship if he could help it. He correctly deduced that salvation lay in the sanctuary of arctic ice-flows rather than travelling at the rear end of a convoy, doing a mere twelve knots. The canny Dutch skipper didn't fancy being tail-end Charlie himself.

A mile or two away to port, an enemy submarine surfaced and gave chase attempting to cut across the frigate's path. If the Lord above were neutral in this latest skirmish,

Mother Nature, at least, was now on the side of the converted frigate and her crew. The U-boat was unable to match her speed in the heavy seas, and was soon forced to give up the chase.

A last desperate salvo of gunfire fell short of its mark. The sub then submerged and was seen no more.

Carol and the crew were now completely alone on the high seas. The Dutch Captain gave orders for his ship to continue heading North. He had decided to break away from the convoy and seek refuge among the icebergs. A decision that not only proved to be a good one by the fact that both cargo and crew arrived safely back in England, but it also afforded all aboard many days of serenity, and a much needed respite.

★ ★ ★

And now, here I was, deathly seasick but still able to appreciate scenes of unforgettable beauty, where mighty and magnificent icebergs seemed to pacify the wrath of the stormy seas. The few times when the skies cleared, the sun shone with a clarity and brilliance seen only in the far north. Particles of ice, of all shapes and sizes transformed in the dazzling sunlight assumed the appearance of dancers bedecked in jewels rocking and rolling on the ocean swell.

It was our last day aboard and we were fast approaching Southampton harbour.

Although still very weak, I was up and ready to disembark. Unfortunately, Hans was on duty and despite it being May, I felt cold and miserable as the morning sun was unable to penetrate the masses of dark grey clouds.

As the ship finally docked, I walked gingerly down the gangplank and my feet finally touched land. I turned and took one last look at the *HMS Sheffield*, the ship that had brought me back to an unknown future.

Suddenly I noticed a figure high above me, his arm waving goodbye. It was Hans. My eyes became misty as I waved back.

Turning away, I realised that I was now completely alone. And I thought: 'Jesus, where do I belong? Where in tarnation do I go from here?'

This unusual story vividly describes the pre-war life of Hugo Bergström at the Actor's Orphanage. The book commences with his institutionalisation at Langley Hall in 1935. Instigated by its new president, Noel Coward, the orphanage relocates to Silverlands, and the story goes on to describe the onset of war, and the resulting evacuation of the children to the USA, where they finally arrive at another institution in New York.

This is a true tale of adventure about boys and girls, coping with pain and joy, laughter and tears, where well-known and unknown people touched their lives.

'A story written with flare, and with the perspective of a child's innocence. The flow of the author's pen is dictated by his heart.'
Paula Adimick, Editor of the Canada Post

We do hope that you have enjoyed reading this large print book.

Did you know that all of our titles are available for purchase?

We publish a wide range of high quality large print books including:
Romances, Mysteries, Classics
General Fiction
Non Fiction and Westerns

Special interest titles available in large print are:
The Little Oxford Dictionary
Music Book
Song Book
Hymn Book
Service Book

Also available from us courtesy of Oxford University Press:
Young Readers' Dictionary
(large print edition)
Young Readers' Thesaurus
(large print edition)

For further information or a free brochure, please contact us at:
Ulverscroft Large Print Books Ltd.,
The Green, Bradgate Road, Anstey,
Leicester, LE7 7FU, England.
Tel: (00 44) 0116 236 4325
Fax: (00 44) 0116 234 0205

Other titles in the
Ulverscroft Large Print Series:

DEAD FISH

Ruth Carrington

Dr Geoffrey Quinn arrives home to find his children missing, the charred remains of his wife's body in the boiler and Chief Superintendent Manning waiting to arrest him for her murder. Alison Hope, attractive and determined, is briefed to defend him. Quinn claims he is innocent, but Alison is not so sure. The background becomes increasingly murky as she penetrates a wealthy and ruthless circle who cannot risk their secrets — sexual perversion, drugs, blackmail, illegal arms dealing and major fraud — coming to light. Can Alison unravel the mystery in time to save Quinn?

MY FATHER'S HOUSE

Kathleen Conlon

'Your father has another woman'. Nine-year-old Anna Blake is only mildly surprised when a schoolfriend lets drop this piece of information. And when her father finally leaves home to live with Olivia in Hampstead, that place becomes, for Anna, the epitome of sinful glamour. But Hampstead, though welcoming, is not home. So Anna, now in her teens, sets out to find a place where she can really belong. At first she thinks love may be the answer, and certainly Jonathon — and Raymond — and Jake, have a devastating effect on her life. But can anyone really supply what she needs?

GHOSTLY MURDERS

P. C. Doherty

When Chaucer's Canterbury pilgrims pass a deserted village, the sight of its decaying church provokes the poor Priest to tears. When they take shelter, he tells a tale of ancient evil, greed, devilish murder and chilling hauntings . . . There was once a young man, Philip Trumpington, who was appointed parish priest of a pleasant village with an old church, built many centuries earlier. However, Philip soon discovers that the church and presbytery are haunted. A great and ancient evil pervades, which must be brought into the light, resolved and reparation made. But the price is great . . .

BLOODTIDE

Bill Knox

When the Fishery Protection cruiser MARLIN was ordered to the Port Ard area off the north-west Scottish coast, Chief Officer Webb Carrick soon discovered that an old shipmate of Captain Shannon had been killed in a strange accident before they arrived. A drowned frogman, a reticent Russian officer and a dare-devil young fisherman were only a few of the ingredients to come together as Carrick tried to discover the truth. The key to it all was as deadly as it was unexpected.